TEMPERAMENT
AND PENMANSHIP

TEMPERAMENT
AND PENMANSHIP

Edited with an Introduction by
Devon James

WHITLOCK PUBLISHING
ALFRED, NEW YORK

Character Indicated by Handwriting first published 1877

First Whitlock Publishing edition 2017

Whitlock Publishing
whitlockpublishing.com

Editorial matter © Devon James
ISBN 978-1-943115-21-1

This book was set in Adobe Garamond Pro on 55# acid-free paper
that meets ANSI standards for archival quality.

ACKNOWLEDGEMENTS

A huge thanks to

Dr. Allen Grove

Ms. Cassidy Weese

Laurie McFadden

Amanda Cross

Alfred University Libraries

Pennsylvania State University Libraries

NOTE ON THE TEXT

During the editing process, misspellings were fixed. Punctuation was amended as well. Traditional British spellings were left unchanged. Most images have been transferred over to similar places in the text.

CONTENTS

BIBLIOGRAPHY

The Witches' Dream Book and Fortune Teller
by A. H. Noe
1885

A Victorian Grimoire: Romance – Enchantment – Magic
by Patricia Telesco
1992

Sex, Lies, and Handwriting
by Michelle Dresbold
2008

TIMELINE

322 B.C.E.: Aristotle discovered a treatise on palmistry at the altar of Hermes that was later presented to Alexander the Great, who took interest in exploring the lines of the hands of people in his life.

The Middle Ages: Palmistry is actively suppressed by the Catholic Church as a superstition.

The Renaissance: Palmistry was classified as a forbidden art in Renaissance magic.

1837: Queen Victoria ascends the throne.

1840: Rhoda Broughton, Welsh novelist, is born.

1839: Palmistry experienced a revival in the "modern era," beginning with Captain Casimir Stanislas D'Arpentigny's La Chirognomie.

1842: Marie-Anne Le Normand, a notable 19th century palmist, dies.

1867: Broughton publishes *Cometh Up as a Flower*.

1877: *Character Indicated by Handwriting* by Rosa Baughan is published.

1886: Broughton publishes *Doctor Cupid*.

1887:	Broughton publishes *Not Wisely, But Too Well: A Novel.*
1889:	The Chirological Society of Great Britain is founded in London by Katherine St. Hill. This society aimed to advance to art of palmistry and prevent charlatans from abusing the art.
	Influence of the Stars by Rosa Baughan is published.
1897:	Edgar de Valcourt-Vermont founded the American Chirological Society.
1901:	Queen Victoria dies. Beginning of Edwardian England.
1947:	In *Mickey and the Beanstalk*, Mickey read the giant's palm.
1992:	Palmistry makes an appearance in Season 4 Episode 8 of *The Simpsons* titled "New Kid on the Block."
1999:	*Harry Potter and the Prisoner of Azkaban:* Harry Potter takes a course on divination and dabbles in palmistry.
2010:	Julia Roberts goes for a palm reading session in *Eat Pray Love.*

INTRODUCTION

ROSA BAUGHAN

WITH HER KNACK for writing about the then taboo subjects of palmistry, graphology, and divination, Rosa Baughan has been dazzling readers since the Victorian age. Few women of her time, heck, few authors of her time, dared to touch upon such subjects. With a climate of religious and political unrest, 1890 was not a time for the bizarre.

Baughan was one of the most respected spiritual theorists of the late nineteenth century, leaving her mark by writing a variety of books spanning genres. The oldest child of a man involved in the newspaper business, Rosa Baughan broke free of the confines of her family trade and created a reputation for herself by claiming that life's events are predetermined and can be predicted through handwriting.

THE HISTORY OF GRAPHOLOGY

Juan Huarte de San Juan's 1575 *Examen de ingenios para las ciencias* (*The Examination of Men's Wits*) is the first documented book of handwriting analysis. In his attempt to show the connection between psychology and physiology, Huarte is credited, to this day, with the boldness and originality of these associations.

In approximately 1830, Jean-Hippolyte Michon published his handwriting discoveries after founding Société Graphologique. From 1893 to 1907, Alfred Binet conducted research on the study of handwriting, or what he called "the science of the future." This later came to be what we know today as "graphology."

Post World War I, the examination of handwriting became a common interest across the United States and Europe. Ludwig Klages, a philosopher in Germany during the 1920s, published his findings in *Zeitschrift für Menschenkunde* (*Journal for the Study of Mankind*). Klages, as well as the aforementioned writers, studied real cases of handwriting, just as Baughan did.

Before the mid-twentieth century, graphology didn't have much of a positive reputation. Modern day graphology is used primarily as a criminal investigation tool, as opposed to the Victorian ideal of personality unveiling. In 1982, statistical tests drawn from more than 200 studies concluded that graphologists were incapable of predicting any sort of personality traits for any person. There have also been studies on ethnicity, race, age, nationality, and weight and their relationship to handwriting, ending up with mixed results. The only thing that could be concluded from handwriting was gender. There have been more than a dozen studies done to determine if gender can be determined through handwriting; these studies have average success rates of between 57% and 78%.

Baughan's radical claim that handwriting can ascertain information about one's personality and intelligence was an avant-garde idea during Queen Victoria's reign. Although she admits the French and Germans had studied the assumptions of handwriting before, she makes it clear that no one had studied English handwriting. Baughan and her "team" she has named "we," who we can assume is merely herself, use this treatise to support assertions made about the characters of statesmen, lawyers, soldiers, ecclesiastics, authors, poets, musicians, and actors. In her short lifetime, Baughan was noticed and praised for her fascinating and groundbreaking ideas delving into a realm with which many were unfamiliar.

CHARACTER INDICATED BY HANDWRITING

Baughan published *Character Indicated by Handwriting* in 1877. Graphology is a pseudoscience that analyzes the physical distinctiveness of movements formed by the hand to make inferences of the physiological state of the writer at the time of creation. Modern day scientists believe that graphology's anecdotal evidence and positive testimonials are not a valid tool for personality interpretation, and most empirical studies fail to show validity in any such claims. Graphology has been controversial for more than a century.

In her most popular work of nonfiction, *Character Indicated by Handwriting*, Baughan obtains the signatures of a range of people spanning various occupations and personalities. Baughan identifies characteristics that she believes people of certain occupations possess.

She claims that although handwriting changes, the "thoughtless" handwriting, on a card to a loved one or a mere signature, can identify ardor or vigor in a person. Baughan and her team collected samples from people of various ages to prove that handwriting is indicative of a new "epoch," formed by external changes, or a new job. These changes in handwriting over various periods of a life were the driving force behind her study. The success of this indication, in Baughan's eyes, is where graphology is superior to "the sister science[s] of...palmistry," Baughan's other prominent interest.

RHODA BROUGHTON AND HER WORK

Credited for being the queen of circulating libraries, Rhoda Broughton, a Welsh novelist and short story writer, aided in developing a system very similar to the library we know today. Most people in Victorian England perceived circulating libraries as the provider of novels to a mostly female clientele, although that was not always the case. The difference between circulating libraries and present day libraries is that circulating libraries reflected public demand, leading to larger collections of fiction. Today, most libraries are still filled with fiction, for the demand of the public hasn't changed much. On top of exposing patrons to a larger literary world through the circulating library, Broughton wrote novels known for sensationalism, causing critics to neglect her later, more influential work. These works were all circulated through libraries.

Born in Denbigh, North Wales on November 29th, 1840, Broughton was the daughter of Rev. Delves Broughton. Her taste for literature developed at a young age, and she frequently alluded to Shakespeare in her work. After reading *The Story of Elizabeth* by Anne Isabella Thackeray Ritchie, young Rhoda was so inspired that she produced her own work in six weeks. Broughton submitted her novel to publisher Richard Bentley, who refused her first book on grounds that it was improper material. Part of this dislike towards her writing came from her reputation for creating fast heroines with easy morals, a type of woman not favored at the time. Many held the opinion that her writing was trivial and frivolous.

Not yet defeated, she took parts of her novel to her uncle Sheridan le Fanu, a successful writer himself; he loved the piece and assisted her in publishing her masterpiece and first work, *Not Wisely, But Too Well*. Broughton's first two novels appeared in le Fanu's *Dublin University Magazine*. He thought her so talented, in fact, that he introduced his niece to Richard Bentley, who accepted her second novel, *Cometh Up as a Flower*.

Broughton employed the popular three-decker structure for her first novels, a standard form of publishing for British fiction during the 19th century. Although this format does not even closely resemble the nature of a series as we know it today, it implemented the idea that a novel divided into three parts could create a more anticipatory demand. The income from Part I could also be used to pay for the printing costs of the later volumes of the novel. These books were sold at a higher price than a single volume novel; this high price meant both the publisher and author could make a profit on the comparatively limited sales of books similar in length. Bentley later published the original novel he deemed worthy and accepted, as well as the one he rejected off the bat, both in the three-decker structure.

Broughton and Bentley's professional affiliation lasted until the end of the Bentley publishing house in the late 1890s; the company was taken over by Macmillan. Over the course of 30 years, Broughton had published 14 novels, 10 of which were in three-decker form. Three-decker novels were often republished at a later date as cheaper, single-volume editions to strike interest in a different literary market. Some books did go on to become paperbacks. The hard cover copy was released, then a solid paperback, then a mass marketed paperback. By doing this, publishers grabbed the highest profit margin from the most willing readers, and then lowered the price to score more sales with tighter profit margins.

After the take over, Broughton remained with Macmillan, publishing another six novels with the company. By this time, her popularity was in decline. In a *New York Times* review published May 12, 1906, K. Clark complained that her latest novel was "hard to procure" and wondered why "such a fine writer was so little appreciated."

In 1910, Broughton moved to Stanley, Paul & Co., where she published three additional novels. Broughton's final years were lived at Headington Hill near Oxford, where she died on June 5th, 1920 at 79 years old. The *Times*, originally revolted by her early novels, dismissed them as "sentimental romances" in her obituary. They did mention, however, that they assumed the modern reader would be interested in seeing the type of book forbidden to their grandmother. The modern reader may be unscathed by the sexual content and politically incorrect race and class verbiage.

This book is compiled to provide examples for Baughan's claims about handwriting. Broughton allows us a peek into the mind of a type of intellectual Baughan collected samples from. Though she is known mostly for her fiction, this publication is focusing on her correspondences (i.e. nonfiction) writing. Broughton frequently incorporates humor and sarcasm into her writing. Readers can't discount her humor before considering the constraints of the time period. Through a sassy tone and hidden meaning, these never before published letters show a bit of Broughton's personality and thoughts on state of mind in regards to handwriting.

GRAPHOLOGY TODAY

Although graphology had modest support from the scientific community before the mid-twentieth century, more recent research rejects the validity of graphology as a tool to assess personality and job performance. Today it is considered a pseudoscience. Graphology is primarily used as a recruiting tool to screen job candidates during the preliminary hiring process. Some companies use handwriting as a background check, while some use it to judge education. Though many studies have been done throughout history to decide if handwriting can predict personality traits and job performance, they have been consistently negative.

A 1982 meta-analysis (a statistical analysis that combines the results of multiple scientific studies) drawn from over 200 cases concludes that graphologists were generally incapable to predict any kind of character trait on any temperament test. In a 1987 study, graphologists were unable to predict scores on the Eysenck Personality Questionnaire (a questionnaire to assess the personality traits of a person, a theory based primarily on physiology and genetics) using writing samples from the same people. In a 1988 study, graphologists were unable to predict scores on the Myers-Briggs test using writing samples from the same people.

A broad literature screen done by King and Koehler confirmed dozens of studies showing the geometric aspects of graphology (slant, slope, etc.) are essentially worthless predictors of job performance. Professionals rank graphology alongside astrology, giving them both "zero validity."

In handwriting analysis for criminal purposes, the first known published book was written by Albert S. Osborn; he is considered the father of handwriting analysis in North America. His most influential book, *Questioned Documents*, was published in 1910 and was later heavily revised and published again in 1929. His other books, *The Problem of Proof* (1922), *The Mind of the Juror* (1937), and *Questioned Document Problems* (1944) were all widely acclaimed in both legal and private concerns. Osborn also founded the American Society of Questioned Document Examiners (ASQDE) in 1942.

In recent times, Andrea McNichol has made a name for herself as a hand writing expert. She is no stranger to high profile cases; she was involved in O.J. Simpson's case, as well the murder trails of Ted Bundy. She wrote *Handwriting Analysis: Putting It to Work for You*, which is used by the FBI, other law enforcement agencies, and Fortune 500 companies. McNichol has used her knowledge of handwriting to link penmanship to a certain individual, break down hoaxes, and unveil fraud. She testifies on whether or not a document was written by a particular person.

Usually, we make assumptions about someone's gender based on curly bits on the ends of letters or perhaps the slant of the words. The fact that there is little to no evidence that personality or character traits can be discerned from a person's handwriting may come as a surprise to those who watch or read mystery shows or novels. Television shows often suggest that handwriting can be used to diagnose and identify diseases such as schizophrenia, or traits such as homicidal tendencies. In the end, the studies determined that we are much more likely to decipher if handwriting belongs to a female or a male.

Complications with the study of handwriting include things such as the phenomenon of The Barnum Effect, which makes it difficult to validate methods of personality testing. Phenomena like this describe the observation that "individuals will give high accuracy ratings to descriptions of their personality that supposedly are tailored specifically to them but that are, in fact, vague and general enough to apply to a wide range of people." Think of this as a sort of placebo effect. In the end, research leads us to believe that graphology results may be inaccurate to decipher character traits of an individual, but may be helpful to discern conclusions about the intent of groups of people.

Baughan's work provides an interesting window into the late 19th century. Because science and pseudoscience were still evolving, the public was open to new ideas. With more recent research, these theories have been disproven, leaving them as dated, yet fascinating facts of the past.

CHARACTER INDICATED BY HANDWRITING

Many great thinkers have acknowledged that the handwriting reflects, to a certain extent, the intelligence and character of the writer many great thinkers have acknowledged, but the study of these indications has hitherto been looked upon rather as a matter of sentiment and fancy than as a serious science. Foreigners, both French and German, have, from time to time, occupied themselves on the subject, and even the great Lavater himself gave some attention to it, though only as supplementary to his work on physiognomy. In his "Physiognomical Fragments," he says: "The more I compare different handwritings, the more am I convinced that handwriting is the expression of the character of him who writes. Each nation has its national character of writing, as the physiognomy of each people expresses the most salient points of character in the nation." We, who have given the matter a longer and more careful study than the great physiognomist thought it merited, are quite prepared to endorse that opinion. The graceful "*insouciance*" of the French nation, its dislike of fixed work, and inability to "buckle to" to steady labour are shown in the rounded curves, the long and sloping upstrokes and down strokes of the most ordinary type of French writing; the vanity and boastfulness of the nation are shown in the liberal amount of flourish in all the capital letters, and in the exaggerated ornamentation of the signatures of almost all French writers, whilst the delicacy of the lines of the letters, the fineness of the upstrokes and down strokes, are all typical of the grace and refinement for which the nation is celebrated all over the world. The German hardness, practicality, and argumentativeness are all visible to the graphologist in the strange angular twists and upright lines in the cramped ordinary German handwriting. There are, of course, in each nation, infinite varieties to be found, but the salient points of national character are, in both these instances, to us clearly apparent. Although we have studied all varieties, it is from English handwriting we shall

1

give our examples, or at any rate, most of our examples, as being, of course, more interesting to English readers.

That the handwriting really reflects the personality of the writer is evident from the fact that it alters and develops with the intelligence—that it becomes firm when the character strengthens—weak and feeble when the person who writes is ill—agitated and erratic when he is under the influence of great joy, grief, or any other passion. The dissimulating, the obstinate, the idle man, all aptitudes bad or good, all sensations, even those that are most fugitive, are betrayed to the graphologist in a simple letter, written, perhaps, with a view of giving its receiver quite a different opinion to that which one learned in the matter would glean from it. We do not, however, go so far as to say that a few lines are sufficient to enable us to give an unerring character of the writer; something we may glean from a simple address or even autograph, but many persons do not form the same letter always in the same manner, and where this is observable, it is necessary to see which form predominates, and from this to strike the balance in the judgment; again, a certain letter indicating, very markedly, a certain quality, may occur very frequently in a few lines, while other letters which the writer might form in such a manner as to indicate an opposing quality (and which, if seen, would modify considerably the judge's views) might not occur even once; or the few lines might have been written in extreme haste or under the influence of some very exceptional circumstances, and thus a character would be given to the handwriting which it would not take in its normal state, or if there had been a sufficient quantity of it for other characteristics to show themselves; of course some salient points in a character may be gleaned from a few lines, or a mere address, but to say that the character of a person may be given in its entirety from such a specimen is to wrong the art.

Neither is it at all fair to a graphologist to send letters for judgment written by persons who know the use to which such letters will be put when the writer insensibly puts himself in position, sits for his mental portrait, and thus his writing becomes unnatural. What we ask is a natural letter, something spontaneous, such as the rough copy of a manuscript, or a letter to an intimate friend, written without any thought beyond putting the ideas into simple and understandable language; a letter, in which the writer had no thought of its being kept or shown about, in which case writing is apt to lose its naturalness, and is, therefore, less valuable as a study. Another difficulty we have to contend with is that we seldom know accurately the character of our most intimate friends, and it thus often happens that the writing being franker than the individual judged, friends are apt to dispute even an accurate judgment. It has, however, often happened to us in such cases that the person so judged has been honest enough to admit to us that we had hit him notwithstanding the denial of his admiring friends. We think that in order to form a thoroughly correct estimate of character from handwriting, specimens should be given from several different periods of life of an individual, for the handwriting changes from youth to manhood, and from manhood to age; although it still retains, even to the most careless observer, something of the same character. As a man is advancing in his career, as he takes up a new position or is led away by some dominant passion, the handwriting takes, in some degree, the forms typical, according to our theory, of these changes. There is nothing to us more interesting than the study of these changes. We come, by comparing different specimens, written at different epochs of the life of the individual to be, at last, able to divine the disposition of mind in which a certain letter has been really written, whatever may be the words in which it is couched. Here is the superiority which graphology has over the sister sciences of phrenology and palmistry. The inquirer has not to ask the person whom he wishes to judge to submit his head or his hand for examination; he has only to write some trivial letter, which shall demand an answer, and, in his reply, the victim offers himself for judgment. As a general rule we avoid taking in the sense of what is expressed in a letter submitted to us for judgment, preferring only to analyse it according to the formation of the letters and their position on the paper, according to our theories on these points. We have sometimes been able to indicate where and at what points of life the writing has taken the typical form of success, or the reverse.

Writing that has a tendency to ascend at the end of each line announces success and prosperity, or, at any rate, that combination in the character of the writer, of ambition, hope, and energy, which would generally lead to success in a career. All, or almost all distinguished generals have this point strongly marked in their writing, as will be seen farther on in the specimen we shall give of the Duke of Wellington's writing from an auto- graph letter now in our possession. A writing, on the contrary, which has a constant tendency to run down at the termination of the lines announces ill [health, or profound melancholy, and therefore a troubled and disappointed life. This descending handwriting, in combination with the signs typical of pride, sensitiveness, and disordered imagination, indicates a tendency to insanity.; but we are forestalling somewhat too much. All these signs will be treated of later, under their several heads, so as to enable our readers to have a regular theory of judgment.

It has been objected (but the objection is almost too absurd to treat) that the various writings we meet with may only be the result of the different styles of each person's writing master, but how then is it that in a school not one child writes precisely like another? Of course the differences will not be so apparent in these childish writings as they will be in the same hands when the writers shall have arrived at manhood; but the germs of ambition, egotism, prodigality, goodness, are all patent to the graphologist, even in these embryo hands. It has also been remarked to us that there are persons who do not often write alike. It may appear so to the ordinary observer, but the salient points,

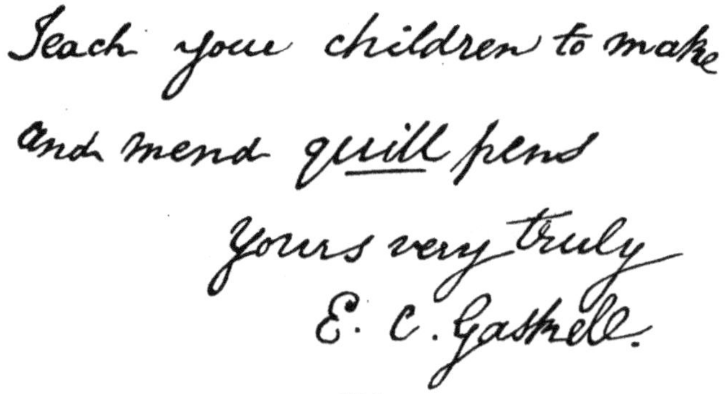

Teach your children to make
and mend quill pens
Yours very truly
E. C. Gaskell.

Fig. 1.

the dominant qualities, will always be there. Again, we have been told with triumph by nonbelievers in our art, that there are such and such persons who can imitate any handwriting. Granted, but we do not think this in the least affects our position; the character then given of such a person's writing would be that of the person whose writing he was, for the time, imitating; but these clever imitators have all their own handwriting, and unless there were some special motive for the deception, it is their natural handwriting they would employ, and by which they would be judged on ordinary occasions. We have also heard it objected that the writing materials used exercise no small influence over the writing. Quill pens give a heavy, firm appearance to the hand,

4

whilst the fine pointed steel pen has the reverse effect. Again we say granted, but the choice of pen to a certain degree indicates character. Few sharp, quick, vivacious persons choose a soft quill pen, while it is seldom that persons of an easy, lazy temperament do not prefer it to the fine pointed steel pen.

In proof of this we will quote a passage from a letter now before us of Mrs. Gaskell, the novelist: — "Please to tell your friend," she writes, "that if I could mend pens my writing would be very much better; but as it is I am driven to use steel, scratchy pens; therefore the moral of this is—' Teach your children to make and mend quill pens.'" We subjoin a fac-simile (Fig. 1) of the last phrase in the letter, with the writer's signature, from which our readers will see that Mrs. Gaskell writes the hand with the full rounded curves, and would prefer, according to our theories, the soft quill, as she says, to the "scratchy" steel pen.

Herr Henge, in his system of graphology, recognises difference of sex in handwriting; but this, we think, is in many cases so impossible that no theory can be formed on the subject which could be at all reliable; as there are men with feminine characters (intellects sometimes those of a very high order—as we shall show), and women who are essentially masculine in mind, so there are handwritings of men which give the idea of a woman's hand, and women whose writing resembles that of a man. From a thousand instances, which have come under our notice, we give the fac-similes of three handwritings, male and female. The first (Fig. 2) is that of Dr. Parkes, one of the first Orientalists we have—a man of high ability, but, probably, of a tender, sensitive nature. Would not this writing, except for the

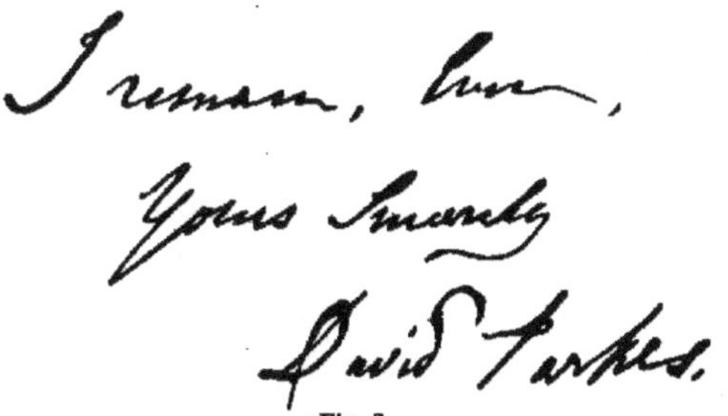

Fig. 2.

male signature, pass well for that of a woman? Whilst the signature of Mme. Dudevant (Fig. 3), the George Sand of French literature, is essentially masculine; and "that of our English writer, Margaret Gatty (Fig. 4), scarcely less so. Having a very valuable collection of autographical letters from distinguished persons of both sexes, we could cite many more instances, but want of space forces us to give

Fig. 3.

only these.

In forming judgments of character from handwriting, we must never forget that we shall occasionally, in our anatomy, come upon the

Fig. 4.

most unaccountable contrasts of qualities. We shall, for example, find traces of great sensibility and even tenderness of heart in the handwriting of persons who may have been guilty of the greatest unkindness and cruelty; but then in these writings there will always be found, on a closer examination, the signs of other and more active qualities, which have dominated and strangled the tenderness. We repeat that to form a correct estimate of character from handwriting we must never lose sight of the existence of these contrasts, which exist in human nature, and which are, therefore, reproduced in handwriting. We must all of us have often come across persons full of tender sympathy in all suffering, whom we yet find difficult to persuade to spend their money on this suffering for which they really seem to feel the most heartfelt pity. Now, in the handwriting of these persons we should probably find the signs typical of avarice side by side with those of sensibility and tenderness, but the former will be the more strongly developed. These contrasts are, as we have said, of constant occurrence, and to the novice in the art offer some difficulties; but each handwriting must be judged as a whole; isolated instances of signs typical of such and such qualities must not be over-estimated; the most frequently recurring type will not for its frequency be sure to be the dominant one, unless the quality suggested by it is a more active one than all the rest, and even then it may be modified by an intermediate quality, as, for instance, great generosity without any prudence degenerates into prodigality, whilst economy increased by egotism becomes avarice. We should ourselves greatly prefer to have dealings with a person in whose writing avarice and tenderness were (both) strongly developed than with one in whose writing we saw only slight indications of possessivity without the signs of tenderness. The first might prove a kind, tender, and sympathetic, though not e, generous friend; the other would, in all probability, be a selfish and cold-hearted companion, whose greed of gain, unsoftened by any tender influences, would induce him to sacrifice his friend, without a remorseful scruple, if, by so doing, he secured his own interests. The handwriting of the late Emperor of the French offered these contradictions. In a letter of his, which we have seen, written in early manhood, during his imprisonment, we remarked the sloping writing, the little rounded and regular curves of the letters, which are to us all indications of a gentle, sensitive, and affectionate nature (which indeed he had to a certain extent), and had it not been for the strongly barred t's (type of determined and energetic will), and the constantly ascending character of the lines (typical of ambition), we should hardly have recognised the writer as the chief actor in the " Coup d'Etat" of some years later. These remarks are of course only preliminary, and, therefore, somewhat discursive; and we shall now proceed to give our readers the details of our theory, with copious examples from the handwritings of various distinguished persons, both of the past and of the present day.

It seems almost a contradiction to begin our theory by an analysis of the finals, but, as we consider them of the utmost importance in the signification they give to the writing, we have determined to explain these differences before giving examples of the different forms of capital letters, Even the most careless of observers must have noticed that, instead of finishing each word with the delicate upstroke so much in favour with writing masters, some persons terminate their words with a brusque, some with an angular, and some with a thick line; that their lines are some- times long, sometimes short—in fact, that there is the greatest possible variety in the manner in which different persons terminate their words in their handwriting. Now these differences have all their various significations to a graphologist and it is our experience of these various significations, which we will now endeavour, as tersely as possible, to explain to our readers as the first step to be mastered in the art. When the finals stop suddenly the moment the letter of the word is formed, as if the writer would not give an atom more ink than necessary, it is an unerring sign of economy carried to the extreme. Should the finals be still more suppressed, then it is sordid economy amounting to avarice. The gradations from honest economy (which is but prudence) to sordid thrift, and thence to avarice, are marked by the greater or less freedom in the length of the finals. When, on the contrary, the finals are long, very ranch rounded and raised, it is the sign typical of generosity. If the finals are not only rounded and raised, but take up along space between the words, are in fact very pronounced, then the generosity becomes prodigality, and should the rest of the writing give a total absence of the signs typical of prudence it would mean extravagance, almost to dishonesty. If the finals are angular and moderately ascendant, and terminate words which have also an ascendant movement, it is the sign of quickness of temper, which is swift to anger—a handwriting where all the finals are well rounded and gentle, and in which there are no broken curves, nothing sudden or sharp, denotes in the writer a gentle, benevolent nature—it is also typical of elegance of mind and perception of form. The writing of musicians of the second order, where imagination is not dominant, is apt to take this form in the finals; this type, in the extreme, is typical of indolence. Finals that are sharply angular, and rising above the level of the other letters, are typical of ardent but somewhat obstinate natures; persons who when they once take up an idea do not easily abandon it.

When the finals take curves which are broken as if the pen had been intended to describe a series of angles, the writers are generally persons with little or no taste for art; it is the sign, unless other points in the letter redeem it, of absence of cultivation, of harshness, and want of tact and sympathy.

We will now proceed to give various examples of the capital letters, explaining, from our experience, what each form signifies to us; we would only observe as a general rule that the more simple the form of the capital the higher order of intelligence does it typify. We will begin alphabetically.

The letter "A" is not to be met with so frequently as other capitals, but it has its significance all the same.

Fig. 5. Robert Burns, the poet (from an autographic copy of the poem of The Cottar's Saturday Night). A most harmonious letter,

Fig. 5.

approaching in form to the printed letter—simplicity, sense of beauty, with will strongly marked in the firm line which crosses the letter; had the capital taken this graceful form with a loop to cross it, the letter would have still been typical of poetic facility, but there would have been less force. Every capital "A" throughout the long poem is formed in exactly the same manner.

Fig. 6.

Fig. 6. Professor Lyon Playfair (in a familiar letter to a friend). A small "a" used as a capital—simplicity, clearness of ideas. Henry Thomas Buckle, the writer, forms his capital "A" in precisely the same manner. There is also sequence of ideas shewn in the stroke leading on to the following letter.

Fig. 7. From a letter of an insignificant person. Pretension and want of grace, shown in the ridiculous and affected flourish of the loop which crosses the letter; a certain amount of imagination and movement in the mind, but an imagination not likely to bear good fruit, being so little guided by good taste. The small letter "a " follows the rules given for the finals as to curves and angles. The letter " B" is of more frequent occurrence 7 than the letter "A" at

Fig. 7.

Fig. 8.

the commencement of a sentence, and there is a greater variety in the forms which it takes; we shall therefore give a few more examples of this letter than of the preceding one.

Fig. 8. The capital "B" in the autograph of Sir Samuel Baker, the great African traveller. Originality, as shown in the eccentric form of the letter, the base being so disproportionate with the head of Fig.8- the letter; great tenacity of purpose, shown in the angular lines of the letter.

Fig. 9. From a letter of Father Newman to an intimate friend.

A cultivated intelligence, as shown in the graceful and harmonious curves, high intelligence, and poetic feeling.

Fig. 10. Ruskin (taken from one of a series of familiar letters to a young lady friend). Ardent imagination, amounting almost to eccentricity, a little pretension, and some conceit.

Fig. 11. From a Frenchman's letter. A great deal of pretension and affectation, as shown in the numerous flourshes, but a certain kindliness and easiness of temper are denoted by the rounded forms.

Fig. 12. Buckle, the historian, from his signature. Absence of affectation, much cultivation, and extreme clearness of ideas, shown by the simple form of the letter, the absence of all flourish, but not so much poetic feeling as in Father Newman's capital, which has more graceful curves, whilst still preserving the simple form of the letter.

The small "b" follows the rules for terminations. The capital letter "C" is one to which especial attention should be directed in studying a handwriting, as it lends itself to indications of vulgarity, pretension, exaggeration, and vanity, more than most letters.

Fig. 13. Gordon Cumming's (from the signature of a short letter accepting an invitation). An unharmonious letter, wanting in proportions, shews imagination and ardour, activity of mind, and vivacity.

Fig. 9.

Fig. 10.

Fig. 11.

Fig. 12.

Fig. 13.

Fig. 14.

Fig. 14. From a letter of Lord Palmerston, sending a voucher to a Captain Cannon. Taste, cultivation, intelligence, as shown by the rounded and graceful lines, and the absence of any excessive flourish.

Fig. 15. Sydney Dobell (from a familiar letter to a friend). Great poetic feeling, love of art; the other letters of this handwriting show extreme imagination and nervous susceptibility: these qualities, with the harmonious form of the "C," would indicate poetic faculty of a high order. His autograph will be given further on among the poets.

Fig. 15.

Fig. 16.

Fig. 17.

Fig. 18.

Fig. 19.

Fig. 16. From a letter from a lady, a third-rate musician, who imagines herself a second Malibran. Unbridled imagination, with insufferable affectation and pretension; the rest of the writing in the letter is in the same style, without one redeeming quality. The letter "D" is one which, like the fore- going, lends itself to an immoderate amount of flourish, and is therefore one in which affectation and pretension show themselves.

Fig. 17. From the autograph of Lord Denman, on a franked letter. Originality and acuteness, intelligence of a high order, tenacity of ideas, as shown by the angular lines.

Fig. 18. The late Bishop of Winchester, Wilberforce (from a short letter to a friend). Sequence of ideas, as shown by the line of the "D" leading on to the next letter; this quality shows itself in several places in this short letter. This "D," from its ease and simplicity, indicates a cultivated intelligence and good taste. In the letter "D" the small letter s have also a great significance; we shall, therefore, give two examples of these various formations, and describe what they indicate.

Fig. 19. The small letter "d" in the writing of an Italian music

11

Fig. 20.

master. Imagination, shown in the eccentric form, and excess of vanity shown by the absurd flourish, always a sign of conceit.

Fig. 20. Florence Nightingale (in a short letter accompanying a report of hers to the War Office, in 1858). A great contrast to the preceding; tenderness and generosity, and sweetness; the first indicated by the sloping line of the upstroke, the last by the rounded and gracious curves of the final. The capital letter "E" is not so characteristic as the letters of which we have been writing, but the small "e," from being so often a final, has a great importance in graphology. We will give two of each.

Fig. 21.

Fig. 21. Archdeacon Sinclair (from a private letter). Extreme originality, shown in the eccentric form of the head of the letter, tenacity of purpose in the angularity often base. The rest of the handwriting shows kindliness and sensitiveness, and great lucidity of ideas; there is, moreover, a continual downward tendency in the lines which argues delicate health or profound melancholy. The signature is clear and devoid of all affectation and flourish.

Fig. 22.

Fig. 22. Charles Kingsley (from the address at the head of a letter to a friend). Cultivation and poetic feeling, indications of originality in the form of the head of the letter. Mr. Kingsley's handwriting is remarkably characteristic of the man, but, as we shall have to speak of it again under other heads of our subject, we will not further discuss it here.

Fig. 23.

Fig. 23. From a letter of a

naval officer who died young. Imagination and ardour shown by the extraordinary upward movement of the final of the letter; these extrav-

Fig. 24.

agantly long strokes upwards show an almost foolhardy disregard of danger—this, with the constantly ascendant lines, is seen in the handwriting of most military men who have achieved a position; it is also, to a certain extent, to be seen in the handwriting of Miss Florence Nightingale, who certainly has shown a noble, though not perhaps m foolhardy, disregard of life.

Fig. 24. A small "e" terminating in this form, angularly, and with several broken lines, denotes extreme finesse. The letter "F" is still less

Fig. 25.   Fig. 26.

frequently met with than the capital "B," and is therefore of less importance.

Fig. 25. The capital letter as seen in the signature of Charles; James Fox. Originality, imagination, and a certain lazy indifference in the rounded curve of the flying stroke at the top; had it been angular it would have been simple vivacity and ardour; most of the terminations in Fox's handwriting have these curved terminations, types of a sort of kindly indolence of nature unless corrected by ascendant lines which in Fox's writing is not the case.

Fig. 26. Mrs. S. C. Hall (from an intimate letter). Cultivation and kindliness; the lines are soft and rounded, and the form graceful. The rest of Mrs. Hall's handwriting denotes, from its sloping lines, sensitiveness; extreme energy and ardour of temperament are shown by the continuously ascendant character of the writing. The letter "G" is one which shows originality or the reverse in its top part, according to the simple or exaggerated lines it may possess; and imagination or the reverse in the lower part.

Fig. 27. Monseigneur Darboy, the Archbishop of Paris, who fell a martyr in the war with the Germans. Goodness and sensibility are shown in the rounded curves of this letter, and firmness and dignity in its decisive lines; no affectation or paltry pretension; it is noble in its simplicity. This letter is taken from the archbishop's signature, and is followed by the words Archeo de Paris.

Fig. 27.

Fig. 28. The great Lord Thurlow (from the address of a letter bearing his frank). Extreme originality in the whole form of the letter; acuteness and great tenacity of purpose, as shown in that thick heavy downstroke terminating with such a heavy angularity. it is not a final, than many other small letters of the alphabet, as the formation of the terminating downstroke is capable of giving very decided indications of the character and aptitudes of the writer; for example, if the downstroke is long and sloping, with a graceful curving return leading on to the next letter, such a form would denote a sweet, sensitive, and tender nature, with much sequence of ideas. If, on the contrary, it terminated angularly, it would indicate penetration; if with a short rounded curve, a kindly but not sensitive nature, with much tenacity of purpose; a long downstroke, terminating in a straight line, thicker at its base, indicates an iron will; if with a straight line, with no return stroke and quite fine at its termination, it would denote economy amounting to parsimoniousness.

Fig. 28.

The letter "H" is one of those, from the formation of which, in a hand- writing, it is easiest to distinguish artistic aptitudes. We do not, however, mean to say, when we point out a certain form of letter as indicative of poetic feeling in the writer, that, from it, we glean that he has actually produced poetry, but merely that the perception of poetry—that artistic feeling—is there. A person may never have written a line of poetry, never handled a pencil, never composed a bar of music, and yet possess, and that in a high degree, artistic feeling which, if combined with a certain ardour necessary to form creative power, would have forced itself into the outward expression of one or other of the arts. We have noticed that the artistic formation of any capital letter in combination with ardour and sensitiveness indicates success in music, either as a composer or an executant, whilst the same form of letter with other signs in the writing announcing observation (which is perception of form) as well as ardour and imagination, the artistic feeling will find its expression rather in painting or in the sister arts of sculpture and architecture than in either music or verse. The artistic form of the letter H (as of all other letters, only that this lends itself, as we have said, more particularly to this type) is that which most nearly approaches the simplicity and clearness of the printed form without losing the grace and flow of the written letter.

Fig. 29.

Fig. 29. The first letter "H" given as an example is taken from the address of a letter from Gerald Massey, the poet, to a lady who had written to ask his permission to set one of his exquisitely graceful lyrics to music. The address at the head of this letter is 12, Henderson-row, Edinburgh, and it is the letter "H" in the word Henderson of which we give a fac-simile. Here we have the artistic form of the letter in its flowing and harmonious lines, which, notwithstanding their grace, still preserve the clearness and simplicity of outline of the printed letter, whilst the imagination of the writer shows itself in the rather eccentric downward curve of the terminating line. Of course one such letter, even if it were constantly recurrent, would not determine one to believe the writer a person of strong imagination; the same types must appear in other capitals or in the finals of the words. In this short, courteous note of Gerald Massey's there are still more conspicuous indications of the imaginative faculty in the other capital letters; the letter terminates thus: —"If any alterations are necessary to make the verses singable I would be glad to make them, but most of my songs have not been written with music in mind." To us the last phrase is almost superfluous in- formation—a writing so strongly indicative of imagination (which is one of the highest intellectual qualities) would lead us to divine that the writer's artistic perceptions would find voice in poetry—the most intellectual of all the arts—rather than in music.

Fig. 30.

Fig. 31.

Fig. 82.

Fig. 83.

Fig. 30. Taken from the concluding lines of a letter of Frith, the artist. Here we have the artistic form in its severest simplicity. Such a letter indicates precision of form, but with- 30- out sensitiveness or imagination, and were it not that the rest of the writing shows signs of both these qualities, we should have felt at a loss to account for the originality, tenderness and pathos of some of this artist's pictures.

Fig. 31. Is the letter "H" in the signature of Henry V. of France, known to the world as the Comte de Chambord. The two lines of the letter, so closely compressed as to be disproportionately narrow and high, denote a certain weakness and inertia, the result, probably, of the painfully false position in which this descendant of a long line of kings has, for years, found himself placed. There is sensitiveness in the sloping lines of this letter, but an utter want of energy and prompt decision; while at the same time the termination in a single thick line indicates obstinacy of purpose; once his decision is made he is not likely to be moved to another course of action. Constraint and suffering are both apparent in the lines of this letter.

Fig. 32. Lord John Russell, from the address on a letter to the Rev. C. H. Hartshorne. Here we have extreme acuteness, as shown in the sharp angular lines of the letter; a certain grace indicates cultivation, that the writer is a man of letters, whilst tenacity of purpose, almost to obstinacy, is shown by the thickened and almost blunted termination of both the strokes in the letter quite guiltless of any rounded or softening curve.

The small letter "h" follows the rules we have given for finals, when it closes a word. We would, however, remark that, where the small "h" in the centre of words has an upward tendency, with a long flowing loop which attaches it in its descent to the other letters, we have found it

Fig. 34.

Fig. 35.

Fig. 36.

denotes sensitiveness and volubility of speech, almost to garrulity. The letter "I" follows most of the rules laid down for the preceding letter, of which it seems to be in form the first part. When the letter is in graceful lines, without exaggeration in the size of the head, it denotes grace, and a sense of the beautiful.

Fig. 33. Here we have the letter "I," taken from a fac-simile of one found in Boileau's handwriting to a friend. The rounded lines denote a certain appreciation of the beautiful, and the clear out- line lucidity of ideas; there is, however, no imagination in this letter.

Fig. 34. From a hurried and intimate letter of the Hon. Mrs. Leigh (Lord Byron's sister), to a friend on a very private matter. Here we have extreme grace, denoting very pronounced artistic feeling; the letter, too, is sloping, indicating sensitiveness. The other capital letters in this short note show much ardour and imagination, amounting almost to eccentricity.

Fig. 35. From a letter of Sophie Cruvelli, the singer. A combination of artistic perception, ardour, and eccentricity, grace and sense of beauty in the sloping and gently curved down stroke, eccentricity and ardour in the disproportionately large head to the letter, force of character and obstinate will in the sudden and /thick line of the first upstroke, almost square at its starting point.

Fig. 36. Richard Cobden, the politician (from a letter, written in 1862, to a friend excusing himself from attendance at a meeting at which his presence had been requested). Strong will in the sharp decided downstroke, no grace, no artistic feeling of any sort. There is' a great deal of movement in the rest of the writing, and force of will is indicated in various ways. The small letter "i" has not much signification, except as a final, when it follows all the rules given for finals. The capital letter "J" so resembles the letter "I" in all points, that it seems almost needless to give examples of it. According to whether the heads and terminations of letters are in proportion or out of proportion with the rest of the writing, so are they types of grace or eccentricity.

In Fig. 37, for ex ample, we have a letter "J" of Marshal Pelissier, the French general, which is a combination of grace, cultivation, and force; grace in the harmonious curves, cultivation in its finish and rather recherché style, and force in the firm downstroke. As a general rule long and flying upstrokes and downstrokes are always a sign of originality to eccentricity, and of a quick, ardent temperament, more especially when these upstrokes and downstrokes do not slope regularly with the rest of the writing. When upstrokes and downstrokes are long, and take regular sloping and harmonious carves, it is a sign of sensitiveness rather than ardour.

Fig. 37.

The small letter "j" follows all the rules for finals, but shades of character may be gleaned from the manner in which the dots are placed over the small letters of "i" and "j." If the dots are evenly placed, neatly rounded, and rather close than not to the letter, the writer is careful, cautious, and calm; if, on the contrary, the dots are flying away from the letter, and of hurried, angular shapes, the writer is probably of a careless, quick, ardent temperament; but, of course, as we have before said, one indication of a certain character is not enough, but it will generally be seen that where there is much movement (that is, where upstrokes and downstrokes fly about in all directions) the dots of the letters"i" and "j" will follow suit. In such a writing, ardour almost to recklessness and imagination are the prevailing characteristics.

The letter " k" follows all the rules for the letter "h," both as regards the capital and the small letter.

The letter "L" is one which, we have noticed, occurs very often in a handwriting on any subject, and for this reason requires careful study. It lends itself especially to flourishing lines, and therefore is very treacherous to pretentious and egotistical people, as it betrays their folly more readily than some of the other letters. A vain egotistical girl, whose Christian name begins with L, invariably writes the letter which, to her small mind, represents her charming self, with an inordinate amount of flourish both as regards the head of the letter and the terminating loop, the end of which she would probably allow to go flourishing

Fig. 38.

down amongst the other letters in the line beneath. We have seen a signature of a "Louisa" of this character where the terminating loop of the capital L went down beneath the line and then was allowed to float aloft, descending only to form the leading onto the other letters of her self-honoured name. We did not form a high opinion of this young lady from her signature

Fig. 39.

Fig. 38. The letter "L" in the signature of the late Duke of Leinster. Extreme grace and cultivation in the harmonious and flowing lines, a little self- assertion in the somewhat disproportionate size of the loop at the base of the letter, but the rest of the signature is full of noble simplicity; the sloping lines announce tenderness, the firm yet delicately crossed "t," a sufficiently strong, but not an obstinate will; whilst the dot of the "i," triangular rather than round, and flying far above and not in a direct line with its letter, indicates the ardour and impatience of the Irish character.

Fig. 40.

Fig 39. The letter "L," which occurs only once in a long letter from the poet George Crabbe to his eldest son. Tenderness in the sloping lines, not much force of character, bat acuteness of observation in the angular loop; the rest of the writing expresses kindness and goodness, but there is not the imaginative power which we found so strongly indicated in Gerald Massey's letter. However we think that those of our readers to whom " Crabbe's Poems" are known, will agree with us that while they abound in observation and tenderness, they are not of a highly imaginative order.

Fig. 41.

Fig. 40. The "L" in the signature of Lord Lucan. Originality, enthusiasm, and ardour, with a strong and determined will. The originality shows itself in the peculiar formation of the letter, which is as much like a capital " S" as the letter it is intended to represent; ardour is shown in the dash and movement of it, and in its angular top, whilst the strong will asserts itself in the heavy square line which terminates the letter. A fine military signature, and the little line under the rest of the letters indicates the caution in which, without this, this signature would be deficient.

Fig. 42.

Fig. 41. A capital "L" from a letter of Lammenais. Extreme originality, almost eccentricity; there is a little pretension in the disproportionate size of the head of the letter, there is acuteness of observation in the angular lines. The small letter "1" follows the rules of the other small letters; we would only observe that any amount of flourish before the loop of the small "1"when it begins a word shows pretension and want of taste. The letter "m" is one, which requires a great deal of study, and which repays it,

Fig. 43.

for it is one, which betrays much to the graphologist. It takes so many different forms in different writings, and there is a great significance in the relative heights of the points in this and the sister letter "n" which should be attentively observed. So many and varied are the types of this letter that one could almost devote a whole chapter to it did space allow it. As it is, our readers will observe we have been obliged to give twice as many examples of it as we have done of the other letters of the alphabet.

Fig. 44.

Fig. 42. The letter "M" on a card of Mr. Adams, the gifted writer of the exquisite allegory, "The Shadow of the Gross." Grace, cultivation, and tenderness. The rest of the writing on the card, which bears simply his name and that of his college, has the same character.

Fig. 43. The "M" in the signature of Monokton Milnes, the poet; inequality in the height of the points of the "M " decreasing in height in the second and third points, a sign of a genius which does not attain its ideal. There is always a slight descent in the points, especially where the letter is formed of three instead of two points, hut this, it will be seen, is remarkable in this particular, the third point being no higher than the small letters in the signature. The rest of the writing (a short note asking a friend to breakfast) shows observation, sensitiveness, and a certain originality. We have reproduced the whole signature, as it repeats "M." The letter "R" is singularly graceful and poetic.

Fig. 45.

Fig. 44. The letter "M" is the handwriting of a woman of fashion: total want of sequence in ideas, considerable obstinacy—not by any means an interesting or pleasant companion we should think. The whole of the writing bears the same impress. It will be remarked that the three points are almost equal; she has attained her ideal, but it was probably not a very high one.

Fig. 45. The " M" in the commencement of a letter of Balsir Chatterton, the well-known harpist: here we have an harmonious letter, grace and tenderness shown in the sloping down- strokes, sure sign of a certain softness and tenderness in the writer. We have rarely seen a handwriting of a distinguished musician without this sign, more or less strongly expressed, of sensitive tenderness, and although we do not quite indorse our great poet's assertion that:

The man that hath no music in his soul,
That is not moved by concord of sweet sounds,
Is fit for treasons, stratagems, and spoils;

Fig. 46.

still from our studies in calligraphy we are inclined to believe
that, while the musician, "in the
general way," has less intellectual
power than other artists, he has
more of "the milk of human kindness " in his nature. We would
remark in regard to this letter " M
" of Mr. Balsir Chatterton, that
where the letter is composed of
three points, what we advanced as regards the disproportionate heights
of the points as showing an ideal not attained does not apply so forcibly
as where the letter is composed of two points only; there is generally in
these three pointed letters a slight depression of the two last points, and
in this example scarcely more so than the form of the letter requires. In
Monckton Milnes' capital "M" the disproportion is remarkable, and

Fig. 47.

thus indicates an intellect, which
falls short of its own ideal.

Fig. 46. From a letter of General
Cambronne. How different is this
large irregular letter from the graceful, tender, and harmonious one of
the musician. Here we have all the
fire and energy necessary for the military career. This letter has much of
the character of Lord Lucan's capitals. The second point rising above
the first is a sign of energy and satisfied ambition, the rounded form of
the points shows a certain gentleness, and the sloping line of the letter
some tenderness, but both these signs are tempered by the little angular
line at the commencement of the letter, which is a sign of quickness
of temper, and by the thick and decided terminating stroke, sign of a
determined and obstinate will.

Fig. 48.

Fig. 47. From a letter of Jay, the well known preacher. Clearness and sequence of ideas shown in the decided lines and in the rounded curve of the termination of the " M" leading on to the next letter, originality in the unusual form of the commencement of the letter, utter absence of all affectation and pretence, a contented mind, satisfied with its position.

Fig. 49.

We have chosen as our last specimen a letter "M" in a short note from a very insignificant person (Fig. 48), because it is an example of extreme pretension and want of judgment, the first part of the letter is simple enough, and the angularity of the second point shows a certain a acuteness of observation, which is, however, considerably marred by the extravagant flourish of the termination of the letter —larger than the letter itself—which shows a pretentiousness sufficient of itself to lead astray a judgment which might else be good.

The small letter "m" has no significance of itself, and follows the laws for finals. We would, however, remark that where the third stroke of the letter is invariably in a writing much smaller than the first and second point it is a sign of great finesse of character. The letter " N" has not quite the significance of the previous capital in determining character, but it is still worthy of some attention.

Fig. 49. The letter "N" in the signature of Florence Nightingale. Here we have harmony, grace, and sense of the beautiful in the clear and flowing lines—tenderness in its sloping position, and goodness in its rounded curves.

Fig 50. We give, by way of contrast, the capital "N" in the signature of Napoleon I., from a letter to the Princess Borghese. Here

Fig. 50.

we have extreme originality in the whole form of the letters—ardour and quickness of temper in the angular curve, and a despotic will in the thick line of termination. In the rest of the writing there is finesse, amounting to dissimulation, and other signs of a brusque and despotic temper.

Fig. 51. The capital "N" used by the poet Robert Burns taken from an auto- graph copy of the "Cotter's Saturday Night," Artistic feeling in the grace and delicacy of the first part of the letter, imagination in the highflying upstroke. We would remark that all the capitals in Robert Burns' writing resemble Gerald Massey's in the combination we see in them of artistic feeling with imagination, a combination which we have said generally results in finding voice in poetry rather than in the other arts. There is, however, also in Burns' writing the extreme sensitiveness which, as we have said, we generally find in all great musicians'

Fig. 51.

Fig. 52.

writing.

Fig. 52. The letter "N" is the signature of Sir William Newton, the artist. The same artistic feeling as in Burns; no imagination is visible in this letter, but great perception of form, cultivation, and sense of beauty. This is the prevailing character of the whole of the short note (an answer accepting Captain Kidd's invitation to dinner), but here and there there are indications of imagination in the finals of the words. The letter "0" as a capital occurs but rarely, and gives but little indication of character. It will be sufficient to say of it that, if large in

Fig. 53.

proportion to the writing, and with an excess of flourish, it denotes a vivid and extravagant imagination; if gracefully formed, sense of poetry and artistic feeling; if angular at its base, penetration, if the curves from the top turn down and lead on to the small letters which make up the word sequence of ideas is indicated. We give but two examples of this letter.

Fig. 53. The signature of the Duke of Ormonde on a franked letter (date 1826), which we give in full. The "O" is harmonious at its base, but eccentric in its first formation, originality. A certain angularity denotes acuteness, sequence of ideas in the liaison of the capital to the next letter.

Fig. 54. The signature of Lord Onslow on a franked letter (date 1828). The capital is extremely harmonious, and indicates sense of the beautiful, cultivation and sequence of ideas, in a very marked degree. When lines are drawn under a signature in a heavy decided manner, as in both these signatures, it denotes caution. The letter " F" has much importance in calligraphy. Like the letter "L," it betrays the pretentions and egotistical person by the facility with which it lends itself to the tendency to flourishes and exuberant ornamentation.

For example: Fig. 55. This letter appears in the signature of Louis Philippe; what egotism and pretension in all those twists and flourishes, so intricate as to cause one to wonder made first, and yet, with all this parade, what a compression, amounting to meanness, there is in the letter — egotism, pretension, and vulgarity of mind are here rampant.

Fig. 54.

25

Fig. 55.   **Fig. 56.**   **Fig. 57.**

Fig. 56. The capital letter "P," in Lord Palmerston's signature, on a franked letter to Lord Normanby. Originality very marked in the large eccentric form of the letter; acuteness in the angular stroke before the commencement of the down stroke. A certain gracious kindliness in the rounded lines of the up stroke and the head of the letter.

Fig. 58.

Fig. 57. The letter "P" on the address of a letter, written by the Countess Dash, the well-known French novelist, to a friend at Paris. Intelligence, originality, and cultivation in the delicate and peculiar form of the letter, a certain tenderness indicated in the sloping lines.

Fig. 58. The capital letter "P" in the writing of a self-made man whose name is, at any rate, as yet unknown to the world at large; we give it as an example, because it expresses so strongly the sentiment of force; boldness, which seeks conflict and self-assertion, are indicated in the great size of the capital _ in proportion to the following letters, and a strong will in the thick and heavy lines in the head of the letter; originality too in the peculiar form. The letter "Q" is seldom seen as a capital, so seldom that, throughout a large collection of more than two hundred autograph letters, we have not come upon one to give as an example: we must, therefore, content ourselves with taking two examples from the handwriting of less distinguished persons.

Fig. 59. From a foreign hotel keeper; originality and imagination are not wanting here, but there is extreme vulgarity in such an excess of ornamentation, and the long line running downwards even after the second, and quite superfluous, loop indicates extreme egotism; this person sees himself and his own interests in everything despite a certain prodigality indicated by the many quite unnecessary linen in the letter.

Fig. 60. From a young lady's letter, goodness and grace in the harmonious curves but no imagination or originality. The capital "R" is worthy of much study for it not only lends itself to the flourishes which suggest egotism, self assertion, and pretension, but it is almost as capable of indicating the gift of artistic perception as the letter "H" which is, as we have already shown a letter in which this quality is more easily discernible than in any other of the alphabet. The capital letter "R," from the many angles which some forms of it may represent, is also capable of indicating, in a very marked manner, the acuteness and powers of penetration of the writer.

Fig. 61, a. The capital "R" in the signature of Lord Ravensworth

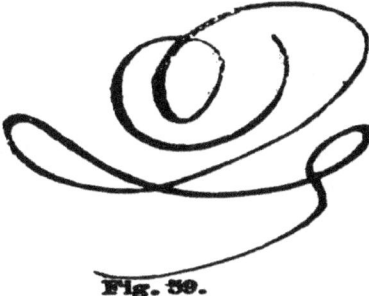

Fig. 59.   Fig. 60.

on a franked letter (date 1839). Sensitiveness is here indicated by the sloping direction of the letter, somewhat neutralized, however, by the two sharp points in the second part of the letter; the rest of the signature (from its sloping and rounded curves) is suggestive of a certain gentle kindliness of nature.

b. The capital "R" of Gounod the composer; a letter, in its simplicity approaching the character of the printed form of the letter—typical of artistic feeling; imagination is suggested (but not that of the highest order) in the head of the letter, which is so much larger in proportion than is usual to the base of the letter. As a rule musicians who are composers, and not mere executants, have the signs typical of imagination as well as those of artistic feeling and sensitiveness in their handwriting. This will be readily understood; the executant is merely the exponent of the composer's creation, what the actor is to the dramatic poet; and, though the creative faculty of imagination is, in some degree, necessary for the complete success of the executant, in either case, we do not generally see it in any remarkable degree in either actor or executant musician. In some of the capitals of Mendelssohn, Meyerbeer, and Rossini we have strong evidences of vivid imagination; but the strongest combinations of imagination and artistic feeling are to be found among the poets, rather than the musicians, as we shall demonstrate when we come to treat of imagination in our examples of writings typical of the various mental and moral qualities.

c. The letter "R" in the signature of Sir Roderick Murchison. The acuteness of the scientific mind is shown in every part of this letter, which seems to be all angles. Here we have no affectation, no pretension, no imagination—acuteness and keen observation dominate everything. The inclined position of the letter, however, shows that a certain tenderness and sensitiveness are not wanting.

d. The letter "R" in the signature of Lord Charles Russell is full of grace and harmony, and might be that of a poet, musician, or painter. The whole signature is beautiful, and, therefore, we have given it in full. There are slight indications of imagination in the head of the letter "R"— artistic feeling and cultivation in its graceful curves sequence of ideas in its liaison with the letter, which follows. The letter "S" is well worthy o£ study, as it not only occurs frequently in the course of a letter, but it is expressive of various types of character and intellect.

e. For originality amounting to eccentricity we do not think the capital "S" we have given from the writing of Cruikshank is to be surpassed. It occurs in the first line of a long letter addressed to Samuel Prince. There is sensitiveness in the sloping position of the letter, and its length, running into the letters of the other line, announces generosity to prodigality. A careless, eccentric, but not untender nature, with much originality, would be our verdict of the man from this letter; but, of course, in judging of a handwriting, every letter must be examined, every dot to an "i," every turn of an upstroke or downstroke, must be taken into account. The large angular splother of a dot to the "i" in the word "Sir "means a careless prodigality.

f. The late Sir Charles Eastlake's capital "S " in a familiar letter to a friend about the sending in of pictures to the Academy. Extreme grace and artistic feeling, but little or no imagination; there is a great sense of the beautiful throughout the handwriting of this letter, great lucidity of ideas, and much tenderness of nature. The signature is beautiful, and devoid of the least shadow of pretension or egotism.

g. The capital " S " in a letter of the Bishop of Chester (Dr. Jacobson) to a clergyman of his diocese. This letter, so clear in its form, and

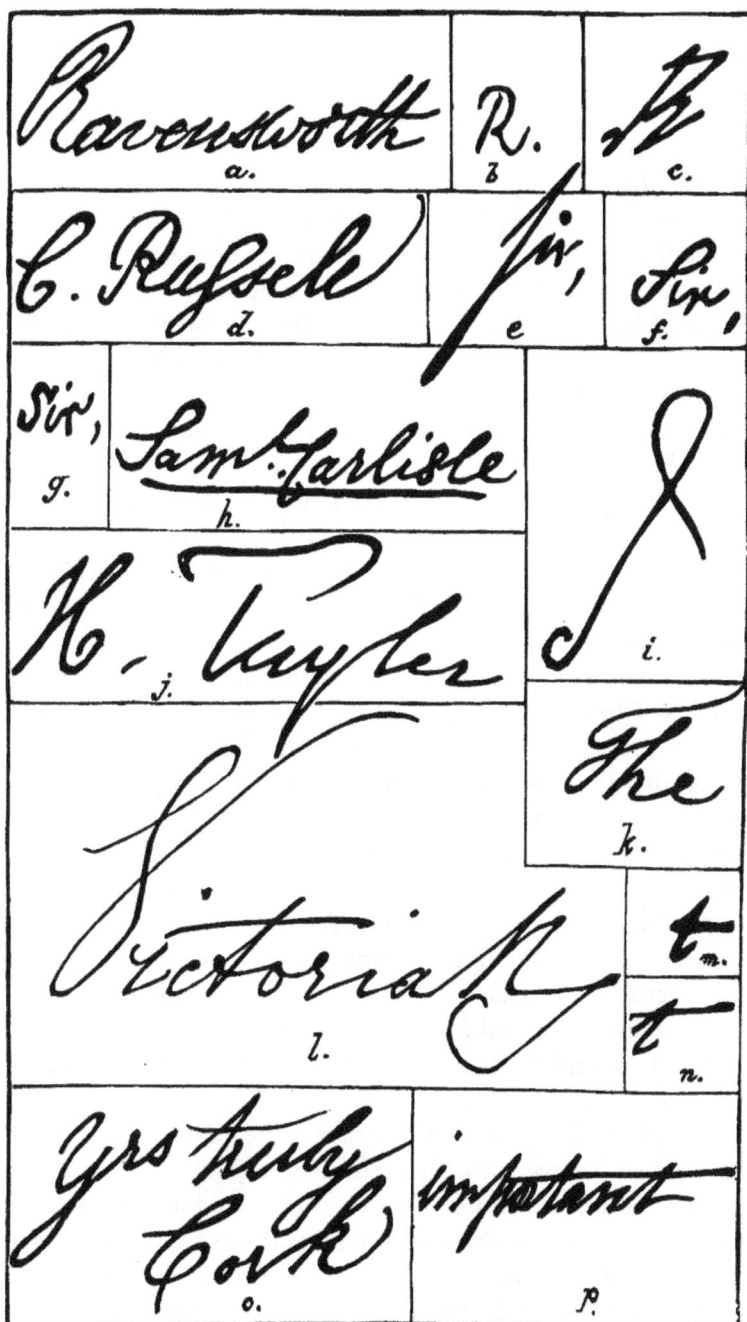

FIG. 61.

29

so closely following the outline of the printed letter, denotes simplicity of taste almost to severity; absence of all pretension; great lucidity is shown by the rest of the writing, which is remarkable for its clearness. The capital letter "S," however, which closes the letter, has not the same form. This variation of form of the same letter in a handwriting may always be taken as indicative of a certain indecision of character. Should it occur only once in a long letter, whilst all the other examples of the letter in question bear the same character, the one exception may be taken as accidental, but where the variation is of frequent occurrence indecision is clearly indicated. In the letter before us there are but these two examples of the capital letter "S;" the second "S," however, in the bishop's letter has, from its unornamental form, much the same character of simplicity and absence of pretence as the first, only it has more tenderness from being less severe in its lines.

h. The "S" in the signature of the Christian name of the Bishop of Carlisle—cultivation in the harmonious lines, force in its decision of form. The whole signature is valuable as typical of the qualities of lucidity and benevolence— the former shown in the extreme clearness of the hand- writing, the latter in its rounded curves. There is caution as well as attention to detail shown by the two dots under the abbreviation of the Christian name, and decision and strong will in the firm, heavy line beneath the whole of the signature. The capital letter "T" is not altogether insignificant in a handwriting, but it has not the same interest for the graphologist as the small letter "t," which is one of great importance, in consequence of the variety of types of volition indicated by the various ways of barring the letter. From the faint and almost imperceptible bar drawn by the hands of persons of little or no volition to the enormous, thick, and sometimes squarely-terminating bars of despotic natures, the small letter "t" receives all the movements of the will and betrays them to the graphologist. We will, however, give two examples of the capital letter before passing on to the more important small letter.

i. A capital "T" in the signature of the celebrated Mrs. Thistlethwayte, the well-known extempore female preacher. Great eccentricity, ardour, and enthusiasm (caused by an imagination but little governed by reason) are shown in the strangely proportioned letter, and prodigality in the wild flow of ink visible in the downstroke. The whole of the writing in the letter has the same character, and a total disregard of opinion is shown in the defiant lines.

j. Here is another rather erratic capital " T " in the signature of Henry Taylor the poet; much imagination in the line of the head of the letter, flying so wildly over the downstroke, but not so much grace and sense of the beautiful as we should have expected in the writing of the author of "Philip von Artevelt." In the letter "H," however, which precedes the surname, the form typical of artistic feeling is very pronounced. fc. The capital letter "T" on the superscription of a letter of Prince Albert's to Lord John Russell, grace, harmony, sense of the beautiful, are here indicated, and benevolence and gentleness in the soft rounded curves of the smaller letters.

l. The small letter "t" in the signature of "the first lady in the land." We have here a strong and long line crossing the " t," and terminating in a thicker point—extreme energy and a will to match. We have given the whole signature, which is truly regal in its noble clearness and the per. feet absence of all petty pretension. The capital letter shows originality and imagination in its peculiar form, as does the capital letter "R" at the termination of the signature. There is artistic feeling in the graceful loops of the capital letter "V." The downstroke of the "g" in Regina shows, like the long bar of the letter "t," will and energy combined, in its decided line; and quickness of temper, and a certain economy are evidenced by its angular curve. The well-known sensitive tenderness of our Queen's nature does not appear in this example, which is probably only Her Majesty's official signature.

m. An example of the small letter "t," from the late Emperor Nicholas of Russia's handwriting; a "t" strongly barred, which gives the character of absolute despotism, intensified by the thickness of the stroke which, it will be remarked, is even heavier than the downstroke which it crosses.

n. The small letter "t" in the writing of General Moreau, taken from a letter written by him to an intimate friend. Here we have in this small letter, which is strongly barred, and very near the summit of the letter, though not above it (in which case it would have quite another signification), an indication of despotic will; this man, if his handwriting presented no re- deeming traits of tenderness and gentleness, would be a domestic tyrant.

o. We have here in Lord Cork's writing a small letter " t" expressive of the reverse of the two preceding examples. A small letter "t" barred with a light and slender line, growing finer towards its termination, indicating a feeble will and a total want of energy in the character, and

31

as the rest of the signature shows extreme tenderness and gentleness, this weak volition has nothing to correct it in point of force in any other quality. There is a great deal of elegance and cultivation of mind suggested by the graceful and rounded curves of the capital letter "C," and in the whole formation of the small letter "k."

p. The small "t" in the letter of an unknown person, but we give it as an example of a letter crossed very low—a sign typical of choleric will, more especially if prolonged and cutting (as is seen in this example) the tops of the lower letters. This person is one to be avoided in his anger. When the letter "t" is barred by long strokes flying far above the letter, so far above as not even to touch its summit, it means a vivacious, ardent, but not obstinate will. A bar crushed down upon the letter, but short and thick, indicates a will both absolute and obstinate. When the stroke finishes by a sort of little crooked line somewhat resembling a hook, it increases the signification of the boldness of the stroke, and suggests a will as tenacious and obstinate as the short heavy low bar, only there is, in such a case, a greater quickness of temper. Persons who habitually bar their small letter "t" in this fashion are not, we should say, the pleasantest members of a family circle.

The letter "U" is very seldom seen employed as a capital, but it would follow (when used) the rules by which we have judged all the preceding letters; that is imagination and originality would be shown in any disproportionate or eccentric forms of the head of the letter, artistic feeling and cultivation in harmonious and simple lines and tenderness and sensitiveness where the letter takes a sloping form; acuteness of observation is capable of being indicated by the lower curves of the letter which, if both terminated in sharp angles, would denote that extreme penetration and acuteness of investigation which we generally find in the writing of all scientific men, and which is also one of the characteristics (although not so markedly) in the handwriting of most of our most distinguished doctors.

The letter "V" is also of very rare occurrence as a capital, but, when employed as such, it lends itself to indications of imagination and originality in a very marked manner.

In Fig. 62 the capital letter " V" in the signature of the late Madame Vestris, the well known actress. There is originality and ranch ardour in the form of the letter, there is also grace in the flowing lines, and a certain tenderness in the sloping direction of the letter.

Fig. 63. Here is a capital "V" of a very different character; it is

32

Fig. 62.

from the termination of a letter written by the late Dr. Chambers to a patient. Absence of all affectation in the simple lines without any pretension or flourish; kindliness in its rounded curves, sequence of ideas in its loop leading on to the next letter, the doctor's acuteness is not shown in this letter, but this quality (which as we have said is always indicated in the writing of all distinguished medical men) is distinctly shown in the angular form of the small letters "r" and "y" in the rest of the word given.

Of the small, letter "v" we would remark that, if the loop with which the letter terminates, connects it with the letter following it it is a sign of sequence of ideas; if, on the contrary, the loop flies wildly in

Fig. 63.

the air above the other letters in the line, it would indicate a vivid, but ill regulated imagination.

The letter "W" has much the same importance in graphology as the capital letter " M," and, therefore, of it we shall give several examples.

The small letter "w" follows all the rules we have given for the other small letters; it would have the same significance as the small letters "m" and "n," but that, as it seldom, if ever, occurs as a final, as the two

Fig. 64.

letters above named so frequently do, it has not quite the same value to the graphologist.

Fig. 64. The capital letter "W" of Mr. Pitt, the great Tory minister, taken from the address of a letter (franked by Pitt himself) to the Rev. M. Walford. Here we have sensitiveness in the sloping lines, cultivation in the grace and simplicity of the form of the letter, and a penetrating judgment in the angular form of the two points in the base of the let-

Fig. 65.

ter; we have given the rest of the name of the person to whom the letter was addressed, as we think the writing so remarkably indicative of the noble clearness of mind and rectitude of character which were the strong characteristics of the great Tory minister; the ascendant movement of the writing is indicative of ambition.

Fig. 65. The capital letter "W" in the signature of Whewell, the astronomer, author of "The Plurality of Worlds," indicates great originality. The letter is unique in form, more like a capital letter "V" than the letter for which it is intended; the acute penetration of the scientific mind is clearly indicated in the angular base of the letter, and also in the sharp point with which it starts off; the rest of the signature expresses extreme lucidity of thought, for the writing, though small, is very clear, and sequence of ideas is shown by the liaison of the capital

letter "W" by a loop to the next letter, which is an unusual form in this letter, though we frequently see it in a capital letter "V."

Fig. 66. The capital "W" in the signature of another great scientific luminary, Professor Wheatstone, taken from a letter written to a

Fig. 66.

friend on scientific subjects; in the initial letter of his name we find great sense of form in the harmonious lines and rounded curves, but no signs of the acute penetration which we see in the form of the same letter in his brother in science, Whewell. There is, however, if anything, more lucidity of ideas in the clear delicate lines of the letters in the sig- nature; there is also great sequence of ideas in the manner in which (throughout every word in the long letter of two pages from which this example is taken) each letter is connected with the one which follows it. Where letters in the same word are constantly divided, it is a sure sign of a judgment intuitive, rather than reasoning.

Fig. 67. The letter "X " as a capital is of still less frequent occurrence than the letter "W," and, in our whole collection, we have not

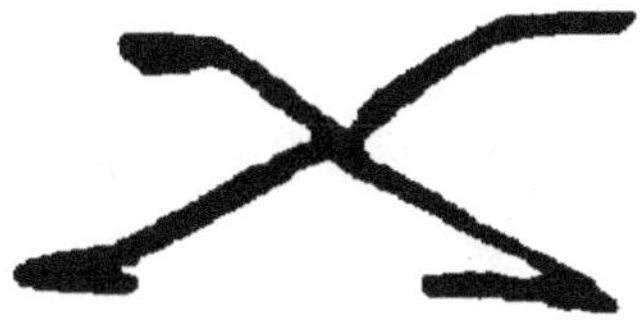

Fig. 67.

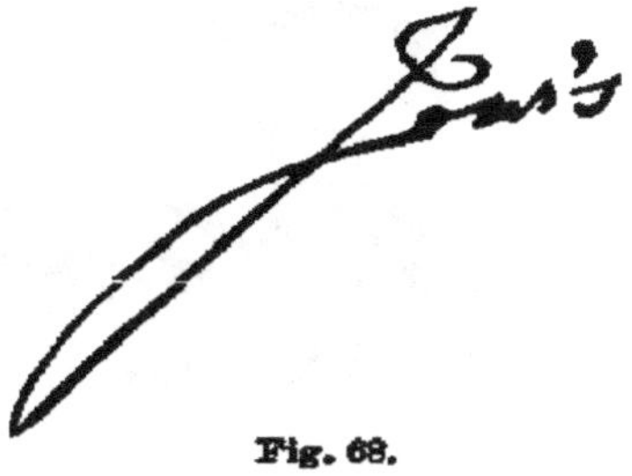

Fig. 68.

a single example of it in the handwriting of any celebrated person to offer to our readers; when, however, it does occur at the commencement of a word it follows the rules given for the capital "W."

We have given one example of the letter from the writing of a person of no note, but from the eccentric form of the letter, we thought it worthy of insertion. Such a capital letter "X," approaching so nearly to the printed form of the letter, would indicate a severely correct taste in

35

art, and a certain originality, as it is a form of the letter so rarely used.

The capital "Y" is worthy of study, as from the form both of the head and downstroke much may be gleaned.

Fig. 68. The letter "Y" in the termination of a letter of Lord Fitzhardinge, taken from a familiar letter asking a friend to dine. Here we have extreme originality in the peculiar form of the letter, which is as much like a "J" as the letter for which it is intended. The ardour, energy, and movement which we generally see in the handwriting of distinguished military men, are all shown in this handwriting; ambition, too, in its ascendent character, and the angular form of the apostrophe between the letters "r" and "s" has the same character. The extreme length of the downstroke indicates an ardent imagination.

Fig. 69. A capital "Y" from the termination of a letter of Dr. Lyon Playfair, is another rather eccentrically-formed letter as regards the head; originality, and sequence of ideas, are the marked characteristics of this letter. The signature of this writer is remarkable for its clearness and absence of all pretence and affectation of any kind.

Fig. 70. The capital letter "Y" in the address of a Frenchwoman's letter. Elegance in the harmonious form and rounded curves, but neither originality nor imagination have any place in this person's mind; there are kindliness and gentleness in the rounded lines both of the capital and the following letters.

Fig. 69.  **Fig. 70.**

The small letter "y" has much significance as regards its downstroke. When it terminates with a sharp downstroke line, unrelieved by any curve or return line, it is indicative of extreme economy in the writer, of thrift almost to sordidness; when it terminates in a small sharp crook, that is with a short angular return of the pen, of a hooked form, it is still indicative of an economical turn of mind, but combined with obstinacy— a woman whose handwriting continually showed this form in its small letter "y," would not be a pleasant "menagère." Long

Fig. 71.   **Fig. 72.**

flowing downstrokes, with the return stroke joining the next letter sig-
nify sequence of ideas, and, where the lines all slope in union with the
rest of the writing, a tender sensitive nature with a certain elegance
of mind. If the lines are long, but irregularly so, and wildly running
into the forms of the letters beneath, such movement and disorder in
the writing would indicate it as that of a tender and sensitive natured
person possessing a vivid, but ill regulated imagination. The letter "Z"
is rarely met with as a capital. When it does occur, it is (like the letters
G., C, and L.), one, which leads pretentious and affected people to
betray their weakness. Among the many letters from celebrated persons, which we possess, we have not been able to find one containing a
capital letter "Z." We have, therefore, been obliged to take two examples from letters of more ordinary people.

Fig. 71. We have here an instance of what this letter is capable of
indicating in the way of affectation and pretentions egotism. We should
say that this person (a teacher of dancing) considers herself and her art
of the first importance to everybody. The letter, however, expresses a
certain kindliness in the rounded curves, but its exaggerated flourishes
show want of taste and cultivation, and an undue amount of self-es-
teem. This person has a vulgar and showful taste; but she is, probably,
generous even to prodigality, but that with a degree of boastfulness,
which must make even her kindliness [oppressive to sensitive natures].

Fig. 72. The capital letter "Z" in a young Frenchman's letter, graceful and tender, yet not without a certain power in its firm downstroke;
a certain simplicity in the lines announces sense of form and artistic
feeling; the writer is a sculptor.

Fig. 73. Small "z" in Voltaire's handwriting, firmness in the decided
downstroke and

Imagination in its disproportionately long terminating downstroke.

Fig. 74. Intermediate small "z" in the writing of an artist as yet
unknown to fame, grace and sense of beauty in its harmonious form,
and imagination in its downstroke, which is rather an unusual form of

Fig. 73.    **Fig. 74.**

the small "z."

Having now gone through the whole of the letters, we shall enter upon the signs typical of the different qualities of mind and character in handwritings taken as a whole.

The sign typical of ambition in handwriting is a constantly ascendant movement of the writing. We often, in conjunction with this type, see sensibility, tenderness, and other qualities of all sorts, but, where the writing has this ascendant movement ambition, be the writer's position what it may, will be the ruling passion. Where not only the writing en masse has an ascendant movement, but where each word takes the upward movement also, the quality is still more pronounced. The ascendant writing means also that hope, energy, and ardour are strong in the character of the writer; but ambition cannot exist without the first quality, and is rarely successful without the last two. There may be hopefulness without ambition, but never ambition without hope. In the simply hopeful character the writing has only an ascendant movement at intervals, and certain words here and there run up, whilst the ambitious character is shown by the unfailing ascendant movement of the whole writing.

We have, before remarked that this character is especially seen in the writing of distinguished military and naval men. In the handwriting of the Duke of Wellington, of which we have seen several specimens, we have remarked that this quality is its salient character, although it presents, as we shall show, signs of other qualities.

Distinguished statesmen and diplomatists have all, more or less, this characteristic, but in most of the handwritings of these persons the qualities of acuteness and finesse, amounting almost to dissimulation, are, perhaps, more apparent than ambition.

In Fig. 75. we give the last seven lines of a note from his Grace the Duke of Wellington (dated London, Aug. 7, 1837) to a Mr. Maccarthy. The note runs thus: "The Duke of Wellington presents his

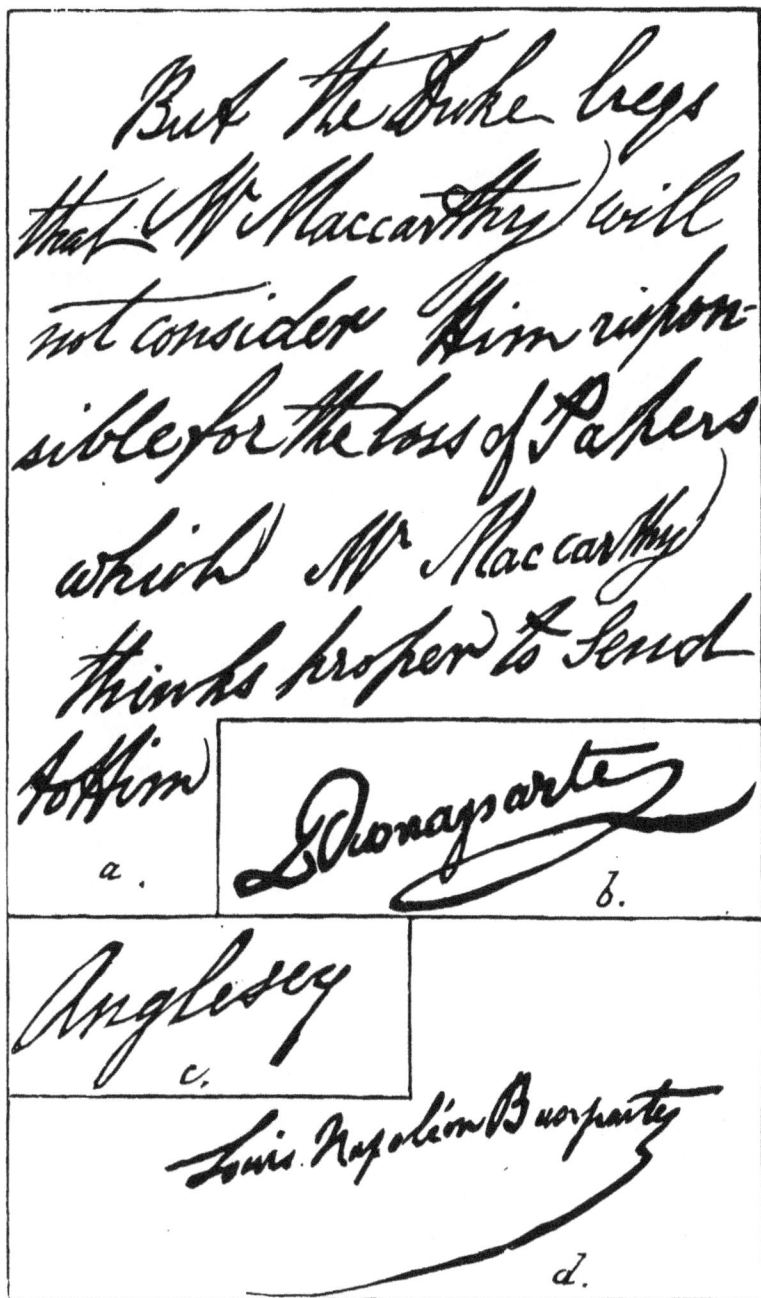

But the Duke begs that Mr Maccarthy will not consider him respon- sible for the loss of Papers which Mr Maccarthy thinks proper to Send to him

a.

b. Bonaparte

c. Anglesey

d. Louis Napoléon Buonparte

Fig. 75.

compliments to Mr. Maccarthy. He has written to him twice already, and has returned his papers. But the Duke begs that Mr. Maccarthy will not consider him responsible for the loss of papers which Mr. Maccarthy thinks proper to send to him."

In this note, the tenour of which shows the Iron Duke's straightforwardness and determination, our readers will see, from its excessively ascendant movement, how dominant was ambition in our great general. The clearness of ideas for which the duke was remarkable is also shown by the spaces left between each word; ardour is shown by the long upstrokes to the terminations of the small letter "y" at the end of the name of his correspondent, which, in both instances, rise far above the line of the writing—a sign, as we have before said, of a reckless ardour which amounts to an almost foolhardy disregard of danger. This is not perhaps a quality we should have thought at all dominant in the waryand sagacious general whose retreats were almost as masterly as his victories, but that this was in his character is borne out by the following extract from the diary of Mme. D'Arblay, written at Brussels at the very time of the momentous battle of Waterloo. "Mr. Saumarez" narration," she writes, "was all triumphant, and his account of the Duke of Wellington must almost have seemed an exaggerated panegyric even if it had painted some warrior in a chivalresque romance. He was everywhere, he said; the eye could turn in no direction that it did not perceive him either at hand or at a distance, galloping to charge the enemy, or darting across the field to issue orders. Every ball seemed fired, and every gun aimed at him, yet nothing touched him; while danger all the while relentlessly environed him, and wounds or death continually robbed him of the services of some one of those who stood nearest to him. But he suffered nothing to check or to engage him that belonged to personal interest or feeling; his entire concentrated attention, exclusive aim, and intense thought, were devoted, impartially,imperturbably, and grandly to the whole—the all." We have quoted the whole paragraph, for it soentirely testifies to what we have said as regards the evidences of reckless ardour shown in this shortnote; still, in giving judgment on this writing, we should say ambition is the dominant character of it,since it is shown in every line, whilst the reckless valour is shown in only three instances.

There is perhaps somewhat of egotism in the capital "H," which the duke puts to the pronoun which represents himself, but a man of such brilliant and world-wide achievements may be pardoned a little self-assertion; besides the duke belonged to a generation which used the capitals more frequently than we do. It will be noticed he writes the noun paper with a capital. His signature, which we have seen but do not possess, is simple enough, but it is rarely to be met with, as it was the duke's custom to write to all but intimate friends in the third person. We would also draw our readers' attention to the relative heights of the two points of the duke's capital letter M in all three instances in which this letter occurs, which, it will be noticed, are both of equal height, a sign typical, as we have before said, of the writer's having attained the height of his ambition; surely this may be said of the Duke of Wellington, " the greatest captain of the age."

b. The signature of Napoleon Buonaparte, in a letter written when only a captain in the French army, but here we have the "vaulting ambition," which made him all but master of Europe. There is the dominant will in the strongly marked "t" and in the hard thick line, which terminates the flourish—his egotism and self-assertion are evidenced in this flourish, his originality in the peculiar form of the capital letter " B," but ambition is here " still the lord of all."

c. The signature of the Marquis of Anglesey, written in 1854, at the age of 86; despite his great age (which generally tones down all the passions) what a markedly salient signature! We have seen another signature in an earlier letter, written in 1845, which has exactly the same character. The angular form of the letters in this signature denotes a quick temper, and, in combination with the hard sharp termination of the letter "y" without any returning stroke, indicates a determined will.

Our fourth and last example of the sign typical of ambition is the signature of Louis Napoleon Buonaparte, late Emperor of the French, taken from a signature of the Emperor's to an official paper. It may be objected that the official signature does not give the character with the same precision as that in a familiar letter. We grant this; but we have seen the signature of the Emperor to a letter of an English friend, and we can vouch for it's having precisely the same character as that of the example given. Ambition, almost as much marked as in his uncle's signature, and the same amount of egotism and self-assertion in the inordinately long termination to the downstroke of the final " e" in the family name. There is, however, more acuteness shown in its angular form than in the rounded form of the same in the signature of Napoleon. The three capital letters show a certain cultivation, which is wanting in the capital "B" of the first Napoleon, which, while showing

41

marked individuality and originality, is quite devoid of cultivation. The signs typical of dissimulation—a serpentine waviness of line (as shown in the word Napoleon, and the first syllable of the surname) are much more discernible here than in the uncle's signature, but the two salient qualities in both men, the colossal ambition and the dominant will, the first evidenced by the ascendant character of the writing, the latter by the strongly barred "t," are equally conspicuous in both signatures.

The signs typical of avarice in a handwriting are as follows:— All the upstrokes and downstrokes of the writing finish abruptly, without any return line; all the small letters terminating each word, have the same character of abruptness and are quite without any prolonged curves or lines, as if the writer could not make up his mind to expend even a little ink unnecessarily. Where these signs are very marked, and where, when they exist, we see no other redeeming signs typical of tenderness or goodness, we should hardly be guilty of a harsh judgment if we decided that such a character of writing denoted the most sordid avarice.

Where these types exist, but in a less marked degree, and where, with them, we see the signs, which to us denote straightforwardness, goodness, gentleness, or tenderness (which will all be explained in due alphabetical course), the writer may be merely of a very economical turn of mind without any shadow of avarice. Our readers will readily understand how many are the degrees between a thrifty desire to make both ends of a small income meet — an honest, although perhaps too rigid economy— and the mean vice of sordid avarice. Possessivity, the desire to amass— the exaggeration of which is misappropriation, or in plain words theft, is shown by the signs typical of economy, in conjunction with those of want of rectitude—the serpentine line of dissimulation, the opposite of straight- forwardness, and the absence of all the signs typical of tenderness or benevolence.

In our first specimen (Fig. 76.) we give a fac-simile of a handwriting in which the most marked character is that of rigid economy, but quite removed from avarice; this writing is that of a lady of high birth and gentle breeding, but who has been forced, from straitened circumstances, throughout her life to look strictly into every minute expense; and, though there is a certain kindliness in the sloping lines of the writing, the habit of having to consider every petty detail of expenditure has made economy a second nature, and it is, therefore, the dominant characteristic of the writing. The little short upstrokes

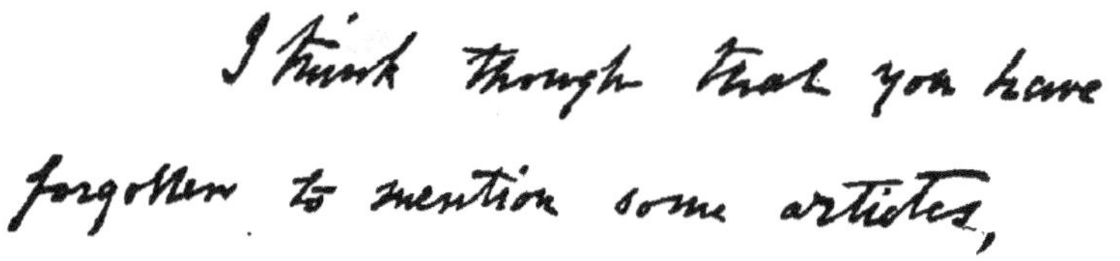
I think though that you have
forgotten to mention some artistes,

Fig. 76.

to all the instances of the small letter "h" throughout the two lines we have given (which our readers will remark are even shorter than the upstrokes of the small letter "t") indicate economy almost to niggardliness; the invariably straight downstroke to all the letters "g" and "y" in the words "though," "you," and "forgotten," the extremely abrupt terminations to the finals of each word are all indicative of a desire to expend as little as possible. There is great lucidity of ideas in this person; for, with such marked indications of economy in the points we have named, it is rather extraordinary to see such a waste of space in the paper. Economical persons generally not only seem to grudge their ink, but their paper also, on their correspondents; for the final letters of their words not only have no curves but finish abruptly, and the words themselves are generally crowded together, as if (as we have said) the writer thought both ink and paper equally valuable. Here, however, another quality in the writer asserts itself—her extreme lucidity of mind, and this a little in this instance over-rides the economy, and thus she leaves clear spaces between her words. Of course, as in all characters there are different shades caused by different combinations, so do we see the same thing repeated in handwritings. To be a clever graphologist requires something of a judicial mind; different qualities must be weighed, and then the balance adjusted. The lady, from whose letter we have taken the two lines of example, is a person of sound judgment, and, did we feel at liberty to give the wording of the letter at full length, our readers would see how clearly, forcibly, and to the point, this person expresses herself; how thoroughly well able she is to see her own interests in business matters, and how utterly unlikely she is ever, by her own imprudence, to become embarrassed in her money matters. There is, however, extreme straight-forwardness in this character, as well as prudence, judgment, and economy; whilst, pushing her own interests to the utmost, she would not do so beyond what she considered to be justly her right.

In our next example (Fig. 77.), we have economy pushed to

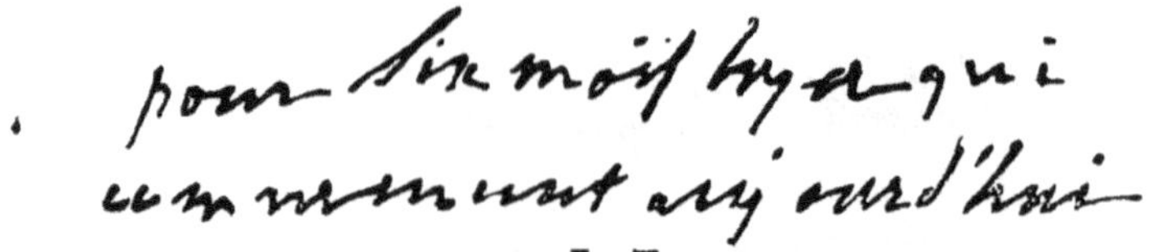

Fig. 77.

avarice; this writing is from the lines taken from the papers of a French priest now dead, who managed, out of the poor income of a curé in an obscure French village, by his parsimony, to acquire sufficient money to render himself the proprietor of nearly a whole street of houses in an adjacent town. The words given are as follows: "pour six mois loger qui commencent aujourd'hui," probably part of a receipt written out by him for some of his ignorant tenants. We would call our readers' attention to the sharp, short downstrokes of the small letter "p," in the first word "pour," the single short stroke which does duty for the letter "j" in the word "aujourd'hui," and above all, to the many breaks in the word "commencent." This man was a real miser; he lived miserably; rarely ever allowing himself more than hard salt bacon and cabbages from his own garden by way of food, and he wrote all his letters on any dirty scraps of paper he found about, a collection of which he always carefully made in all his walks; and yet, as we have said, this man died possessing what, for that poor district, was thought a considerable property, on the proceeds of which he might have led (but for this love of amassing) a life of comparative ease and comfort.

In the last specimen (Fig. 78), which we give of the qualities of avarice and economy, we have a short note from the poet Rogers, the well-known writer of "The Pleasures of Memory." Rogers was one of the few poets who have died rich. Here, again, we have economy, and that to a marked degree, but not avarice—there is a kindliness in the small, delicate, and rather sloping writing which would forbid the extremes of avarice. The finish, grace, and cultivation which are to be found in "The Pleasures of are here indicated by the artistic form of the capital " P" in the first word of the short note, and in both the capitals "S" and " E" in the signature of the letter. The latter letter is singularly harmonious and most forcibly indicative of the poetic feeling shown in Mr. Rogers's poem of "Italy." The quality of thriftiness is clearly evidenced in the absence of any strokes to the finals of the words throughout the little note, and in the abrupt and peculiarly short downstrokes of the letters "y" in the word "pray," the letter "f " in " breakfast," and the

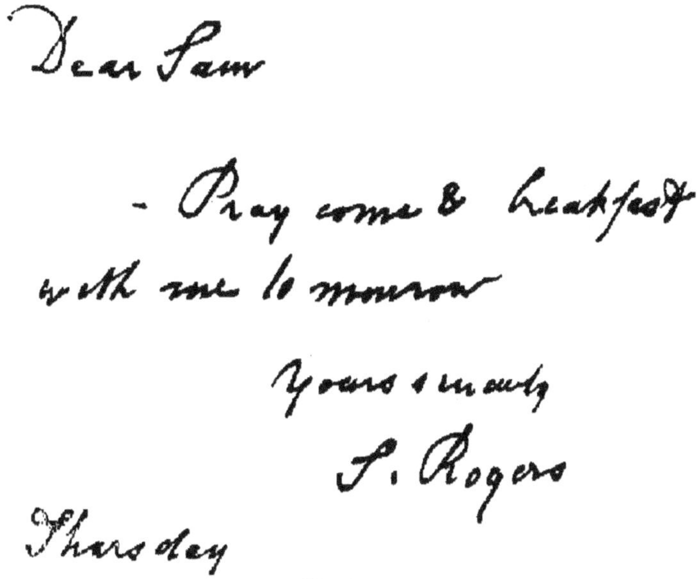
Dear Sam

– Pray come & breakfast
with me tomorrow

Yours sincerely
S. Rogers
Thursday

Fig. 78.

letter "g" in the signature of the poet's surname.

The writing, which is peculiarly significant of benevolence or goodness is a combination of the signs typical of the various qualities of gentleness, tenderness, truthfulness or rectitude (by which we mean truth in action as well as in words) and generosity.

The sign typical of gentleness is negative rather than positive, it being the total absence of those quick and angular forms, both of intermediate and final letters, which belong to the writing of ardent, fiery, and energetic natures.

The quality of tenderness is shown by a sloping writing; hard, cold, and self-contained natures write with almost upright characters; whilst sensitive and tender persons betray themselves as such by inclined lines; such writing, seen from a distance, has the appearance of aspen boughs swayed by the breeze. Where, in combination with this sloping position of the letters, there are the other signs typical of egotism (that is, much flourish in the signature) such a person will be tender and kindly, but of morbidly sensitive tenderness (above all things in matters regarding himself), which makes what is generally known as the "touchy" person; where the writing is very sloping, in connection with a clear and simple signature, the writer will be of a sweet and tenderly sensitive nature, and it is, of course, almost unnecessary to add that it is this type of tenderness in. which, when seen in combination with the other forms typical of generosity and rectitude, will represent to the calligraphist, the quality of benevolence in the writer.

Rectitude (the word has a rectangular sound; but, by it we mean, as we have said, truth in action as well as in words, in point of fact, honour) is typified by a writing in which the lines are straight and equidistant one from the other, and in which all the small letters, both intermediary and final, are of the same height. When the final letters are smaller than those in the commencement of a word it is a sign of finesse, if not of dissimulation, in the writer. Generosity is signified by a writing in which there is a good deal of flow in the finals, the contrary, in fact (as will be easily understood), of what we indicated as the signs typical of avarice.

To resume, benevolence then is indicated by a writing which shows absence of all angular forms, which absence is typical of gentleness; universally sloping letters, indicative of tenderness; even sized letters

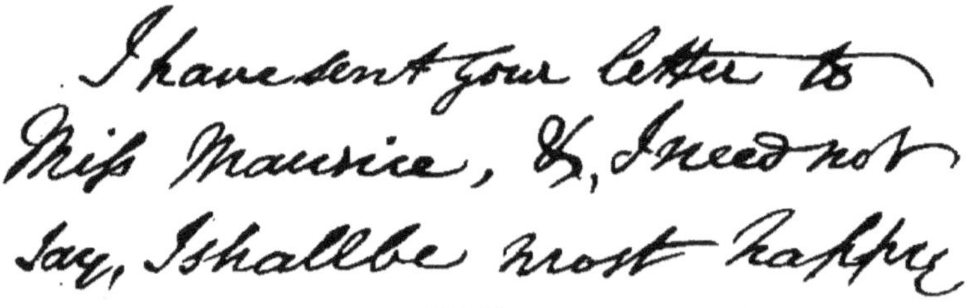

FIG. 79.

in equidistant lines, typical of honour; and the full-flowing finals indicative of generosity. In our first example (Fig. 79), from a letter of Charles Kingsley, the novelist, we have all these signs, as we shall presently show. The letter is one written to an old friend, and runs thus: — "Eversley Rectory, Winchfield, May 29, 1852. My dear Mr. Smith, — Pray forgive my having overlooked your letter through press of business, and two absences from home, which you must know put one's correspondence into arrear where it is large. I have sent your letter to MissMaurice, and 1 need not say I shall be happy if I can be of any service to you in this or any other matter. The sight of your

46

handwriting awoke in me many old recollections. Believe me, yours faithfully, C. Kingsley."

In the three lines of fac-simile we have taken from this letter (the kindliness of which made us quote it at full length) our readers will notice all the qualities we have enumerated as the combination desired to typify benevolence. Gentleness in the absence of all angular forms, tenderness in the sloping direction of the letters, and is not this tenderness fully evidenced by the sympathy with all suffering which his writings show? Rectitude and straightforwardness are shown in the equidistant position of the lines, generosity is indicated in a less degree than in the two other examples we shall give, but it is there in the rounded finals. There is in this writing of Mr. Kingsley's a combination of high moral, as well as intellectual qualities, and (but here we shall, we fear, offend both the clever and the good) such a combination is rather rare, although, in the two other examples we shall give, it will be found equally noticeable. The capital letters, graceful and harmonious in form, show cultivation and poetic feeling, and the signature is sim-

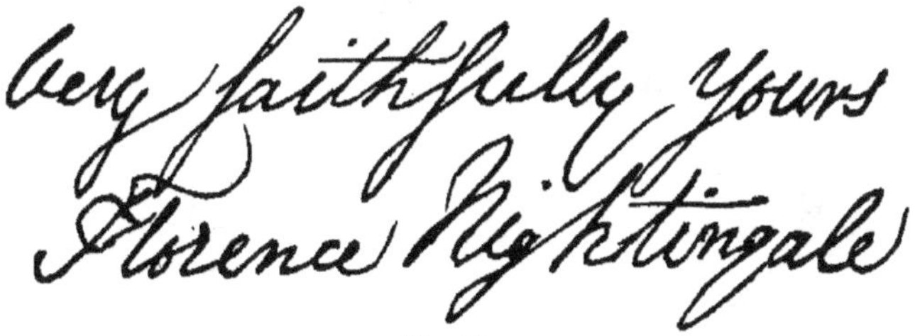

Fig. 80.

ple in the extreme, showing a total absence of egotism or pretension.

In the next example (Fig. 80.) we give two lines; the termination and signature from a letter from Miss Florence Nightingale .to a friend; like Kingsley's, this letter is full of kindly thoughts for others, and run thus:

"Dear Sir, — As we are acquainted with the present editor of the Edinburgh Review, I thought it might, perhaps, be agreeable to you if I procured a list of the authors of the articles in the April number."
Then comes the list, made out with extreme neatness and care; and the concluding paragraph is another instance of active benevolence. "We have at present a page, a Derbyshire boy, who has learnt everything that he can learn under a butler, and is an honest, good boy; should you know of any family who needs such a servant, will you

kindly remember him?" Then comes the termination with the signature, which we have given. Our readers will see how very markedly
prominent is the sign typical of tenderness in the sloping direction of
the writing. The sig-nature is very sweet and simple, and the capital

Fig. 81.

Fig. 82.

letter "F" shows originality.

In Figs. 81 and 82 we have the writing of one of the kindliest and
sweetest natures " that ever lived within the tide of time." Here we
have the soft rounded form perfectly devoid of all angular movement,
denoting gentleness; the sloping lines, which indicate tenderness; and,
most remarkably, the even line of the writing and uniform size of each
letter, indicative of that sensitive, chivalrous sense of honour, which
belonged rather to the past age than to our own; lastly, we have the
prolonged and flowing finals, typical of generosity, in the superscription of the letter, which we have added because it possesses such strong
indications of this quality, which was remarkable in the writer, who was
generous even to prodigality. There is extreme grace, cultivation, and

poetic feeling in the capitals of the opening of the letter — imagination and originality in those of the superscription — yet even the eccentric form of these is softened into harmony by their full rounded curves. Page after page of "copy" have we seen, in days gone by, thrown off in these fair flowing characters, without blot or erasure, but the paper is worn and the ink faded, from which we take these examples. For the heart, which indited the tender words, the slender graceful hand which transcribed them, have been for years in the grave; his—

> Was the doom Heaven gives its favourites,
> Early death—

and those now living who knew and loved him (and to know him was to love him will understand us when we say it seems almost impossible to imagine that tender, genial, pleasure loving, and pleasure-giving nature "grown aged in this world of woe." Had he done so, would he have remained the gentle optimist ho was perhaps the saddest (although at the same time the most interesting) study to the calligraphist is that of the changes which come over a handwriting as circumstances sway the character. How the soft, unformed, childish hand strengthens into the self-assertive lines of early youth, when the writer judges himself from his own estimation before the world has had time to set him right on the subject of his powers; sadder still to note how the sweet serenity of some soft, dreamy, and sensitive nature becomes agitated when the tornado of passion has swept over the life. Saddest of all, when the ascendant writing of some ardent, ambitious, and hopeful spirit becomes depressed, and sinks into the drooping lines of the habitual despondency which the cares and disappointments of life bring to so many of us. All this may seem to be a mere ipse dixit on our part, and, although from a packet of old letters we have been studying we could easily prove what we advance, still such a proof would be in our eyes a sort of treason—a violation of the sanctity of friendship. But this is a study which our readers can make for themselves, for there are few who have not at some time or other in their lives possessed some brother, sister, friend, some alter ego, whose letters were too dear to be destroyed, and every event of whose life was known to them. Let them give an hour's quiet study to some such relics of the past, and we think they will feel the force of what we have advanced.

Candour is indicated (as we have already explained) by a

handwriting in which the letters of the words are all of the same size, and, where the lines are even—that is, do not take the wavy serpentine line—typical of untruth, or at any rate dissimulation. The lines also should be equidistant; it is not, however, necessary that they should be even with the line of the paper, for a person may be truthful and yet have much ardour, hope, and ambition (which are all indicated by an ascendant movement), in which case the writing suggestive of candour would retain all the point we have mentioned, only the lines, while even and equidistant in point of the position of the lines, would take a continually ascendant direction. A writing which presents the salient points indicative of candour without the sloping direction of the letters, typical of tenderness and sensitiveness, would be significative, to the calligraphist, of a straightforward, truthful person who would not hesitate to tell us disagreeable truths; whilst, on the contrary, a sloping handwriting, in which the letters were all the same size, and the lines even and equdistant, would suggest to ns a sweet, frank, and honourable person, who, whilst telling us the truth on all points of importance, would do so in the gentlest and least wounding manner possible.

In Fig. 83, taken from a familiar letter from the ornithologist Mr. MacGillivray (author of "The Rapacious Birds of Great Britain") we have a specimen of extreme candour without the tender sensitiveness,

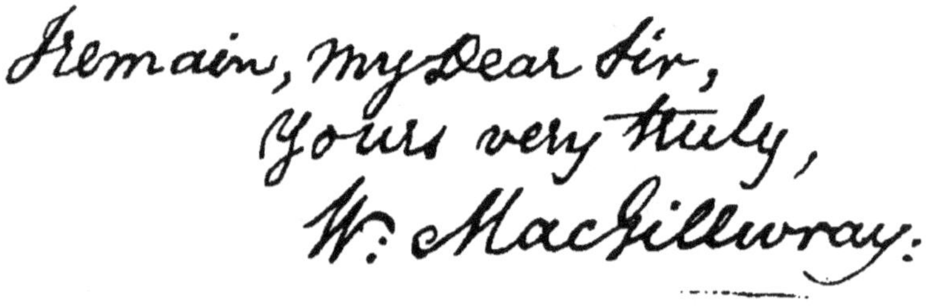
I remain, my Dear Sir,
Yours very truly,
W: MacGillivray.

Fig. 83.

which would withhold unpleasant truths. lhe clearness in this writing is something quite remarkable; there is here great lucidity of ideas, and a certain kindliness, though not sensitiveness, in the rounded curves—a thoroughly trustworthy, straightforward nature, without pretence or egotism of any kind. This is signified by the simple signature, without the suspicion of a flourish discernible. The line under the signature signifies caution, and this quality is also suggested by the exactitude of the punctuation. The letter is dated from Chanomy, Old Aberdeen, Dec. 16, 1843, and runs thus:

"My dear Sir,—I thank you, sincerely, for the trouble you have taken on my behalf respecting the mollusca. If you could send the books to Longman's, addressed to Mr. Alexander Mitchell, Bookseller, Aberdeen, on any Friday afternoon, they would come safely. I am glad to see Zoology so prospering in London. For us in 'the North Countrie' there are only small pickings; I have, recently, got 'Solecustns strigilla-bus' from Stonehaven, and a splendid specimen of Natica helicoides." Then follows the termination we have given. The whole of this letter is written in the same clear round hand, with the lines as equidistant as though they had been ruled by a writing master. There is no originality or imagination in this writing. As a rule, those hands which are remark-

Fig. 84.

able for clearness, frankness, and straightforwardness do not evidence much of either of the qualities we have instanced as wanting in Mr. MacGillivray's writing; and this will be readily understood. Imagina-tion may exist with strong reasoning powers, but such a combination is rare. The judgment of imaginative persons is intuitive, rather than logical, for the exuberance and warmth of creative fancy somewhat precludes the calm necessary to an impartial judgment on any matter.

In Fig. 84, we have candour in conjunction with a remarkable degree of sweetness and tenderness. The writing is clear, evenly spaced, and very sloping, the sign typical of an extreme and sensitive tender-ness. There is no marked originality or imagination in this hand either, but the graceful form of all the capitals is indicative of cultivation and a sense of the beautiful in art of all kinds.

In Fig. 85, we have a very remarkable specimen of the reverse of the qualities we have been discussing. We have thought that (as alpha-betically dissimulation can be treated immediately after candour) it would serve to illustrate our remarks more forcibly if we gave an exam-ple of this quality at the same time as we treat of candour and straight-forwardness, as our readers will thus see the writings in juxtaposition.

51

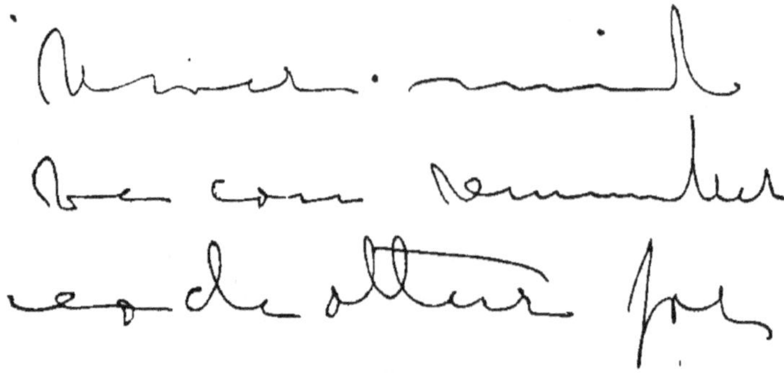

FIG. 85.

same art) to do a service. The promise was given, and our friend (full of hope) brought us the letter from the more fortunate artist who had the power to befriend. We were struck by the remarkable evidences of want of truth in the writing, and observed to our friend, " This person will never do what has been promised." We were thought to be prejudiced, but some months later our friend wrote, 'Handwriting is a surer guide than physiognomy; henceforward, at least, I shall think it so; you were quite right in your prognostication. The person whom you judged, as I thought harshly, has proved false to every promise." The sentence in the example we have given requires interpretation. It is intended to represent these words—"Never mind, we can remember each other for." We would call our readers' attention to the almost threadlike line of the word "mind," and of the centre letter in the word "remember," to the irregular, uneven size of all the letters, and to the serpentine movement of the word "other" in the third line. The letters (so upright as almost to be perpendicular) denote a total absence of tenderness and sensitiveness; a bad combination, and rare in artists of any kind. There are, however, throughout the letter marked signs of extreme originality and imagination in the eccentric form of the capitals. There is also strong will indicated by the fine manner in which the small letters "t" are barred—always a long, strong line, growing thicker at its termination; a sign this of an arbitrary will.

We would, before terminating this portion of our subject, warn our readers against the error of confusing dissimulation, or want of straight- forwardness, with finesse. We use the word finesse in its original sense, that is, in that which it conveys in the French language, from which it has its origin. Finesse is not dissimulation, it is merely that subtleness of mind which enables its possessor to see a thing in all its bearings. It is a quality belonging to clever, rather than to deceptive, persons; indeed, one may be of a very loyal, upright nature, and yet have finesse. The handwriting which indicates this quality is angular, denoting penetration; and the commencing letters of each word are larger than those forming the finals, but (and this is the great point of distinction between finesse and dissimulation) the lines of the writing are straight; the writer wishes to take no unfair advantage, he only wishes to arrive at his ends cleverly, that is all. He does not wish "to do," but only not "to be done;" and there is a great difference.

Energy is typified to the calligraphist by a writing rather angular than rounded, and one which has a somewhat ascendant movement of the lines, though not as markedly so, as in ambition; this is easily understood. Most energetic persons are, to a certain extent, ambitious—eager to arrive at some end or other, whether small or great—which is for the moment the aim of their activity; indeed, in most writings where ambition is the salient point, we generally find also the signs which indicate energy, but still there are some in which they are absent. In such cases (where the writing is very ascendant, with rounded, not angular, curves) a slow determined ambition is indicated, and more especially so where (as is generally the case in such instances) the bars of the small letters "t" are short and thick, suggestive of an obstinate will. Where the lines of the writing take constantly, bat moderately, ascendant "movement, where the letters are angular; and, above all, where the small letter "t" is, wherever it occurs, barred with

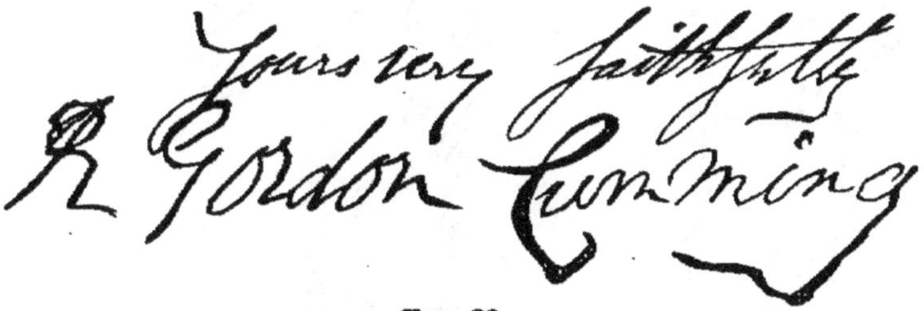

FIG. 86.

a long stroke lying somewhat low on the letters at its first start off, and then taking the ascendant movement of the rest of the writing towards its termination, the writer will be a quick-tempered, energetic person, with quite enough will to make him (combined with his energy) troublesome as an opponent, but he will not be obstinate or despotic. This handwriting is very general among the great travellers. We have it in Sir

Samuel Baker's handwriting, and very markedly so in the example we give in Fig. 86, which is a fac-simile taken from a short note of Gordon Cumming, the lion hunter, to Mr. Gladstone, which has been kindly lent us. The letter is a simple acceptance of an invitation to dinner, and as, although the writing is very original, the matter is not so, we do not transcribe the whole letter. The example we have taken is from the termination of the letter, with the signature, which is very characteristic, as being so full of movement and energy. Our readers will remark in this writing all the points we have indicated as suggestive of energy: first, the somewhat ascendant direction of the lines; next, the angularity of the letters; thirdly, the long bars to the small letters "t" all having the ascendant movement at their termination. Our example (Fig. 87) is from the writing of a private friend of our own -a man of untiring, we might almost say restless, energy. Here we have the ascendant movement still more marked—ambition as well as energy, the long sweeping bars to the small letters "t" are very remarkable, and also the angular form of the letters throughout the writing. We would call our

Fig. 87.

Fig. 86.

54

readers' attention to the unvarying ascendant movement of the long sweeping bars to the small letters "t." This is a very marked indication of extreme energy; not this the nature to linger by the lonely hill side, or to lie dreaming the hours away on the golden sand of some solitary sea-shore, lulled into delicious languor by the monotonous plash of the slowly-ebbing waves; no, " Quiet to quick bosoms is a hell." If he ever meditated what he would call "dawdling the morning away by the sea," he would choose rather the brisk incoming of the tide; and even then he would go down to the shore armed against the possible ennui of the dolce far niente, with an armful of the daily papers. Unlike Fox, who was indolence personified, and who, when a friend suggested that a certain spot in the grounds at St. Anne's would be a charming place for dawdling a morning away with a book, replied, "Yes, very; but why with a book? "Fox's writing (of which we have a very interesting specimen in the shape of a highly characteristic letter) has all the rounded curves and softly looped small letter "t's" indicative of extreme indolence.

When a writing presents the salient points indicative of energy and ardour, like the two examples, combined with indications which are suggestive of imagination, then we have the ardent, energetic, and enthusiastic person. Add to these the slightly sloping writing indicative of tenderness, and we have the energetic and faithful adherent to zeal, even to a hopeless cause. Generosity is indicated by a writing in which there are long rounded curves to all the terminations, and in which the lines and the words are placed wide apart. The writer has no thought of petty economies of paper or ink; all is careless profusion. Of this quality we should have a very good example in the writing we gave in our remarks on " Benevolence; " but, being so rich in valuable autographic letters, we do not think it well to give two examples from the same handwriting. We have, therefore, selected in preference the writing of George Crabbe the poet. Our example (Fig. 88) is taken from the concluding lines of the letter, as we thought the signature would be interesting to our readers. The letter is dated July 21, 1829; it is addressed to his eldest son, and runs thus: "My dear Son, I find that I might have spared myself the trouble of making such long apology for my want of Influence with great men, but I thought it Eight; for certainly it might appear to many that I was placed in the way of Solicitation to those who have Patronage, but enough of this at present. "I want to be with you—I feel every Day a stronger Wish — but why not then come to us immediately? Probably this may appear an easy Question, but I give you my serious and even prompt assurance that it is not. Are you of such importance that your Friends, with whom you have been associated five weeks, cannot or will not part with you? This still is a hard Question, and I cannot answer it with any propriety. But when will yon come? fix the Day: I will, the quickest that it is in my power; in the mean Time pray write and tell me (I hope you can) that you do not think of returning for Weeks to come, how many I cannot say ; but let them be as many as it is possible, and be fully assured that, but for some rather peculiar Circumstances, I would leave Hampstead in two days, and be at Trowbridge in four. In short, 'as I cannot write of all that passes, and ranch less of all I wish and feel, respecting myself and yon, I must trust myself to your Clemency, and that of Caroline. Assure her—indeed you may—that I have Pain and Vexation, in finding Things turn not very different from what I had planned and purposed when I left Trowbridge. Tell her I hope, in my next letter, to mention my Return, with Confidence, and thus it must rest. Ton will believe the Motive strong that keeps me—though most kindly treated where I am — from the place where I would be. Love to Caroline; I do beg of her to take care of herself; right good Care; one of the causes for my Anxiousness to be at Home, is the seeing with my own Eyes that you have all as much Comfort as can be sought and found, in and about your present Residence. I wish I could depend upon you all in this Respect. Love to the dear Girls and Boys." Then come the three lines we have given in fac-simile as our example, and after them the following postscript: " I omit whatever I have thought—and such thoughts continually occur—on our late subject. There is no Time for this, no Place, but I am far, very far from Forgetfulness or Neglect of a subject, to me, so deeply Interesting." We have given this letter, postscript and all, at full length, for the whole wording of the letter is characteristic of the tenderness, benevolence, and generous feeling we find in the simple and sweet style of the poet. There are not any indications of imagination in this writing, but there is a great deal of tenderness(indicated by the sloping direction of the writing), and a certain sense of beauty and poetic feeling in the graceful and simple form of the capitals, of which we have quite a study, for Crabbe followed the old style of placing capital letters to every noun. The quality of honour in the character of a handwriting has almost the same signs as candour, viz., an almost rectangular straightness of the lines, and a perfect equality in the size of the letters. We do not mean to say that the writing need be rectangularly straights regards the paper, but the lines must be rigidly equidistant one from the other. The ascendant movement of the writing indicative of ambition, ardour, and energy may exist, and very frequently does, with

FIG. 89.

the extreme rigidity of equidistsnt lines, in which case the writer would be of an ardent, ambitious temperament, but with a keen sense of honour. We frequently see this combination in the writing of military men. We particularly remember to have noticed it in Lord Lucan's writing and in that of the great French General Moreau. In the two examples (Figs. 89 and 90), which we give, however, the signs typical of ambition are absent. In the first example, which is a fac-simile of the address of a letter from the great Tory minister, William Pitt, to a college friend, we have the signs typical of honour very strongly marked; the line of the writing is remarkably even, and all the letters are the same size; there is cultivation in the graceful and simple forms of the capitals; great lucidity of ideas evidenced in the extreme clearness of this writ-

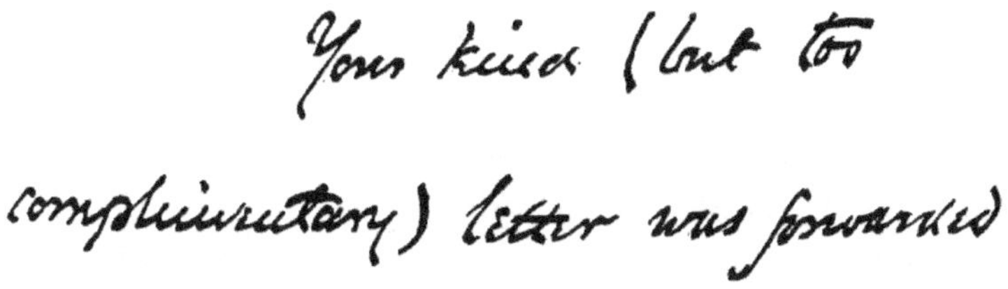

FIG. 90.

ing, and caution is represented by the two strong lines drawn above and below the signature. There is a certain calm serenity in this writing, which announces a judgment not likely to be obscured by ardour or enthusiasm, but tenderness and sensitiveness are indicated by the sloping direction of the signature. In Fig. 90, which is a fac-simile taken from the letter of a private friend of our own—a man of an almost punctilious sense of honour—we have the same character of unswerving honour, the same equidistance of the words in each line, the same equal size of letters in each word; but in this handwriting the will is more strongly indicated; the fine short bars, the same thickness throughout to the small letter "t" in both instances where they occur indicate a strong, almost obstinate will. There is originality in the rather peculiar form of some of the capitals. The wide spaces between each word are indicative of clearness of ideas. The whole writing shows, like that of Pitt, great cultivation. The fac-simile of the handwriting of Pox, we give as presenting, as its salient point, the signs typical of indolence, the rounded languid curves and the absence of all rigidity, both in the direction of the lines and the terminations of the letters. The example (Fig. 91) is a fac-simile of a letter written by Fox on business, in the month of April of the year 1800. How different in character is this

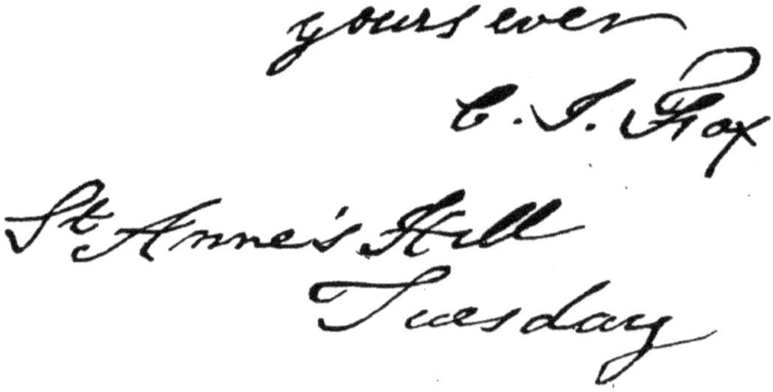

FIG. 91.

writing to that of Pitt! How serpentine the line of the writing in the address! How wanting in energy are all the letters! There is a certain kindliness in the rounded curves, and originality and imagination are demonstrated in the head of the capital letter "F " in the signature. These qualities are also shown in the rather eccentric form of the small letter "x;" total absence of all affectation or pretension is visible in the simple signature; caution is also altogether absent, for throughout the whole of this letter there is not a single stop except after the letters "C." and "J" in the signature. One of the principal signs typical of imagination, as indicated in the hand- writing, is a certain movement, irregularity, and, to a certain extent, illegibility, owing to this very movement. The mind of an imaginative person works rapidly, and the writing takes

the same character: long, flying up strokes and down strokes, terminations of letters flying upwards, and float ing, like banners, over the
other letters, large eccentric forms to the capitals, all these things are
signs of imagination. Still, with all this, the illegibility of the imaginative, must not be confounded with that of the uncultivated writer. We
are far from saying that all illegible hands are those of persons of imagination. The writing of the poetic or imaginative person, with all the
illegibility, and even untidiness peculiar to it, has always the redeeming
point of a certain grace of form in the capital letters, which is (as we
have before asserted in our remarks on the form of capitals) indicative
of artistic feeling or sense of beauty. This, though we find it much more
amongst the writings of artists
and sculptors, is hardly ever
entirely absent from the writing of the poets, although in
these writings the wildness
and movement of the writing,
and consequent illegibility, is
the more salient point. There
are, how ever, some exceptions
amongst the poets in this particular. Tennyson, Browning,
and Gerald Massey, all poets of
no mean order, write perfectly
legible hands; but in all three
the other sign typical of imagination is very strongly indicated, namely, the large and
eccentric form of the capital
letters. This is very remarkable in Gerald Massey's writing (as will be seen when we
give his sig- nature among
those of the poets), but with
all the force and originality
which these large headed letters indicate, there is still a
grace in the form of the full
flowing lines indicating the

Fig. 92.

perception of beauty so necessary to the poet. In Fig. 92 we have given four lines from a long letter of the poet Samuel Taylor Coleridge to his friend Thomas Pringle, the editor of one of the annuals of the day, to which Coleridge had been asked to contribute. The date of the letter is 1833, iust one year before the poet's death; this may, in some measure, account for the want of power—indeed, we may say, the feebleness— of the writing; but our readers will notice the long up strokes and downstrokes, and the rather illegible character of the writing as bearing out what we have said concerning some of the signs typical of the imagination in writing. We would also draw our readers' attention to the total absence of will in this writing; not once is the small letter "t" (when it occurs) either looped or barred. The terminations to the letter "d" in both instances flying over the other letters, show imagination.

Fig. 93. is a fac-simile taken from the conclusion of a letter of Mr. Kinglake's (the brilliant historian of the Crimean War) to ourselves. Imagination is here very dominant, both as regards the long up strokes and down strokes and the illegibility of the writing. This illegibility of the writing of the imaginative must not be confounded with that of the dissimulative person. The want of clearness of the latter grows out of the natural desire of the writer for concealment—to appear what he is not, or rather not to appear what he is; whereas the want of clearness in the writing of the imaginative person is simply from the movement given to the pen from the fervour of ideas which a strong imagination gives. Of course it is rare that a very imaginative person is highly and rigorously truthful—that could hardly be. All imaginative persons view things in the glow of their own minds, and, in that they do so, they are as truthful in expressing facts as they appeared to them as the more coldly judging minds are in their version of them. The sentence we have given, which may be even more illegible when taken off than it appears in the original, runs thus: "It will interest me to have some conversation with yon some day about the mystery of handwriting. "There is sequence of ideas in the liaison of the three words "me," "to," and "have," which appear almost like one word, and strong will is indicated by the heavy thick stroke of the small letter "t" in the word "with." Some of the small letters "t" are not barred; this indicates a will strong on points where the writer feels an interest, but not an arbitrary dogged will—the will of the domestic who must have everything, from his children's education to the folds of his drawing-room curtains, his own way. As a general rnle, where we see signs which have a strong indication of any quality, sometimes much marked, in the same writing side by side with the total absence of such indications here and there, it will always mean that the quality indicated is passagère. For instance, where the flying strokes over the letter "t" indicative of an ardent temper, quick to anger, are only seen here and there; while over other instances of the letter "t" the bar lies calmly across, the writer is quick to anger when fairly roused, but not necessarily always so. These are shades which a calligraphist must be careful to ob- serve, or his diagnosis of a character will some times appear to be far astray. When letters, having no indications of any marked sort, are found made in several different ways by the same writer, it indicates a certain indecision of character. These remarks are par parenthèse; we will now continue our observations on the handwriting in Fig. 93.

Our readers will remark how much movement there is in the down strokes of this writing; for instance, the long loop of the small letter

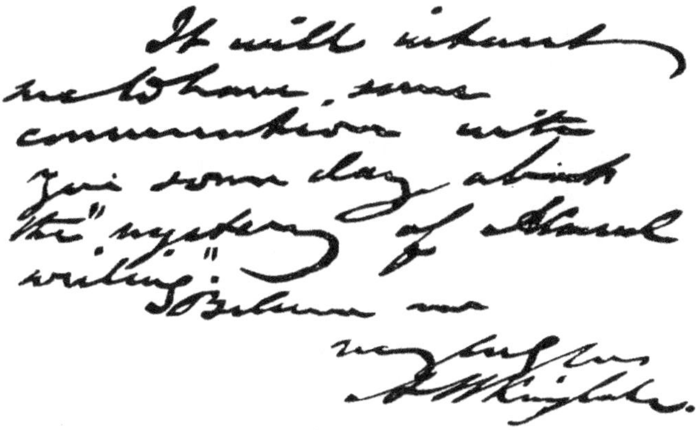
It will interest
me to have some
communication with
you some day about
the "mystery of Hand
writing." Believe me
very truly yours
A W Kinglake.

Fig. 93.

"y" in the termination of the word "day," and the same to the "y" at the end of the word "mystery." We would also draw their attention to those in the line above the signature, where they, in two instances, cut the capital letters beneath them; it is this point of the flying movement of upstroke and down strokes which gives in most cases the illegible character to the writing of imaginative persons; but we must again assure our readers that we do not at all mean to say that all illegible writing shows imagination. Want of cultivation is specially indicated by illegibility, but it is illegibility of a totally different sort. The writing of imaginative persons, considered even from the writing master's point of view, has the redeeming quality of a, certain grace and flow in the lines of the capital letters, which is, on the contrary, always wanting in the writing of persons of no cultivation, where, as a rule, the capital letters are always irregularly ugly, meagre, and devoid of all beauty.

Fig. 94 is a fac-simile of the termination of a letter from Lord Byron's sister, Mrs. Leigh, to a friend. The letter, though very interesting, is of too private a nature to be quoted here, but the signature is very characteristic as indicative of imagination of a very fervid kind. There is grace as well as marked originality in the forms of the capital "A" in this signature, and in the form of the letter "L" there is much imagination. There are many qualities which have no special signs in

FIG. 94.

handwriting, but which are indicated by certain combinations of the special types of other qualities. This we have already noticed in our remarks on benevolence, which, our readers will remember, we showed to be indicated by the combination of the types significative of gentleness, generosity, tenderness, and rectitude. Now, the quality of jealousy, like that of benevolence, is also indicated by a combination of tenderness or sensitiveness (a jealous person is always one of warm affections), egotism (generous persons are not prone to jealousy), and, to a certain extent, imagination. The calmer judgment which goes with the more reasoning minds is rarely disturbed by jealousy.

Trifles, light as air, are to the jealous
Confirmation strong as proofs of Holy Writ.

This is as true as everything else, which the great master in the divine art has said, but it is of itself a proof of how much the imagination has to do with jealousy. We do not mean to infer that all imaginative persons are prone to be the victims of the green-eyed monster, but only that, given a certain amount of imagination, the brooding self-consciousness of egotism and a fair degree of sensitiveness and tenderness, and we have the naturally jealous person. It follows, therefore, according to our theories, that when we see a handwriting which presents the disordered movement and eccentric, though graceful capital letters (typical of imagination), the inclined letters, which always denote a great amount of tenderness, in combination with the flourishes in the signature, which are a sure sign of egotism, we may safl-ly assert that such a person is of a jealous nature. In the hand- writing in Fig. 95 we have all these three qualities—the sensitive tenderness which is rather prone to take offence, in the sloping letters; the vivid imagination (shown by the flying movement of the down strokes), which would be quick to magnify the offence; and in the signature (which is a distinguished one, but which we do not, after what we have said, think it altogether fair to give) we have the egotism which would resent the possible or supposed slight as an offence and deepen mere annoyance into jealousy.

We will not give more examples of this quality, but pass on to that of the sign typical of judgment. In all handwritings typical of this quality the imagination (being, if not the highest, at least one of the highest mental qualities) will always be to a certain extent represented, but rather perhaps by the sign typical of it as rendered by the large and eccentric and graceful capitals than by the movement and illegibility which, as we before said, is the other sign indicative of the imagination, but which is rather that of the fervid, than the cultivated, imagination. Now, as judgment presupposes a certain amount of reasoning power, we shall find, in the handwriting of persons gifted with the high intelligence which gives reasoning power, the other signs typical of clearness and penetration strongly developed; and the imagination dominated, or, at any rate, held in check by these powers does not run riot as in the writing of persons in whose character it is the ruling quality. Still, we rarely see a handwriting of a per- son of high intelligence, either as regards science or logic, without some evidences in it of the existence of the imagination. The imagination suggests hypotheses; reason (which is the combination of lucidity of ideas with penetration) calmly discusses them, and judgment 'is the result. Judgment in a person is typified in two ways in the handwriting: there is the judgment which is the result of intuition, and the judgment which is the result of sequence of ideas. The first is shown by the letters and syllables of a word being all in juxtaposition, but without any connecting lines; this in a handwriting invariably means the faculty of intuitive or instinctive judgment and rapid observation. We see this in the writing of critics, and also in the

Fig. 96.

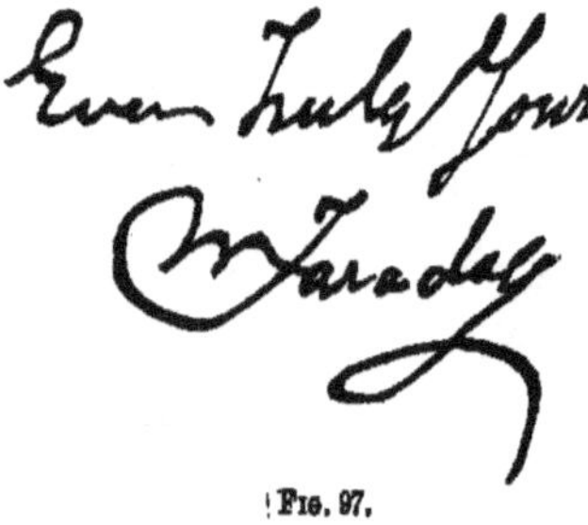

Fig. 97.

writing of novelists who have distinguished themselves in the description of social life and character. In Fig. 96, which is the signature of poor Theophile Gautier, we have a remarkable instance of this faculty of intuitive observation. Those to whom the "lever, immoral, and profoundly melancholy works of this write- are familiar will acknowledge his wonderful powers of observation as regards social life. The signature is remarkable in many ways; there is originality in the small letters placed where there should be the capitals to the name; great imagination in the eccentric long stroke after the last letter of the surname; but the salient quality is the extraordinary amount of intuitive observation shown in the manner in which eaeh letter of the word Gantier has been made with a separate movement of the pen.

In Fig. 97. we have, in the fac-simile of the termination of a letter of Professor Faraday, a specimen of the judgment by sequence of ideas, or deduction. The fac-simile is taken from the termination of a letter from Professor Faraday to Mr. Tennant, and is dated from tie Royal Institution, December, 1855. This writing is remark- able for its clearness, a quality generally seen in all the writings of distinguished scientific per- sons. Imagination, too, is not absent in the form of the capital "M," and in the long termination to the final letter "y"; but the dominant quality is sequence of ideas, as shown in the liaicon of the end of the "y" in the word " truly" with the head of the capital "Y" in the word "Yours." It is also very remarkably indicated by the connecting stroke of the letter "M" with the capital letter "F" in the surname.

In Fig. 98. we have the signature of the Baron Cuvier, the man to, whom natural science owes so much. Here we have another instance of judgment and observation, de- rived from sequence of ideas rather than from intuition. The first two capital letters in this signature lead on to the capital "C" of the surname; the villainous flourish beneath the signature is quite un- worthy, in its pretentious vulgarity, of so

FIG. 98.

65

great a genius; but even this is another instance of the sign typical of sequence of ideas (judgment from deduction), as instead of being a flourish apart from the signature, it is a continuation of the small letter "r" at the termination of the name. There is imagination in the terminating line of the letter "C," but that quality we should expect to find in the writing of a man who has, scientifically, recreated a great number of lost species.

Loyalty is another of the qualities shown by a combination of types, and therefore one of which we need give no example but in words. The handwriting which shows loyalty is one which has the sloping character indicative of tenderness, combined with the rounded curves and full flowing lines of generosity, with the ascendant movement of the lines of the writing which is indicative of ardour and enthusiasm. Given all these indications, with a total absence of egotism, and we have the loyalty which sheds its blood like water even in a failing cause.

The melancholic desponding temperament of disease is indicated by a handwriting the reverse of the ambitious, ardent, and hopeful. Instead of the ascendant lines and upward movement of many words in the line there is a constant depression of the writing—a tendency to run down into the corner of the page; and besides this, certain words will even have a down- ward movement of their own, apart from that of the line. Such hand- writings as these indicate ill health, disappointment, want of success in life. It is true it may be objected that handwritings, having this tendency, are often those of persons who have attained a high position in society, in literature, in science, or art; but even so, it would invariably be found, if we questioned these persons (always, also, supposing they were obliging enough to answer that questioning truthfully and unreservedly) it would always, we repeat, be found that these persons, so apparently successful, had, by some means or other, missed the one thing, which was to them the great good of life. We do not go so far as some of the French and German graphologists do as to say that a descending handwriting indicates fatality, a tragic violent end, although, as we shall presently show, such persons have generally shown this downward tendency in their handwriting or signatures. We do not, in the least, assume the power of diving into futurity beyond that when we see a writing strongly indicative of ambition and ardour, with a strong will and high intelligence, we should feel inclined to prognosticate for the writer a successful career, and of handwriting showing other and opposite qualities, the reverse. When with the descending handwriting, there are also signs of ill-governed imagination, as well as much egotism in the signature, without in the least assuming to ourselves the power of divination, we should say that such a combination would make insanity not only possible, but probable, at some period or other in the life of the writer, because desponding, self-concentrated, and imaginative persons are precisely those whose minds are easiest thrown off the balance by any great crisis whether of joy or of grief.

In our first example (Fig. 99.) we have a fac-simile from a despatch from the Emperor Louis Napoleon to the Empress at Paris. Could any writing be more remarkably descendant than these lines? the ill-success— our foreign brothers in the art would write fatality—which drove him from the height of power to die an exile in England of a painful and lingering disease, is beginning to dawn upon him here. In some earlier letters of his which we have seen (and from one of

FIG. 99.

which we have given his signature), the mounting movement of the lines indicative of ambition, is very marked, but yet here and there, even in these earlier letters, we noticed certain words had a down- ward tendency; where this is the case—we mean where the writing has an upward movement and yet some words here and there descend—it indicates a nature subject to occasional fits of despondency, but not dominated by it I unless where the lines begin lower, gradually ascend towards the middle but again descend before the end of the line; therefore, where the march of the writing describes a sort of arch, it indicates a naturally desponding nature, which struggles against such despondency, but which finally succumbs to its power. We do not know the exact year in which this telegram was written, bat we know, from certain indications, (for we have carefully studied several specimens of the Emperor's writing at different periods of his life) that these hastily scribbled lines must have been very near the time when misfortune seemed to close round him. The finesse and subtlety of his character is shown by the sinuous line of the word "Imperatrice," and again in the word "Boulogne," which is very serpentine in its movements, and caution is shown by the short thick line after the last word to prevent anything more from being added by another's hand. The word Paris, in which many of the letters appear without connecting lines, shows the intuitive judgment for which Louis Napoleon was, like his uncle, remarkable. The hurried accent over the word "a" is not like his usual impassive calm, but this may have been accidental.

In the second example (Fig. 100.) we give the signature of Edward Lear, the clever author of "The Book of Nonsense," from a bright and characteristic letter of his to an intimate friend. There is nothing to indicate melancholy in the letter which we give be- low, but there may yet be, in spite of his success, some disappointment or grief in the life of which the outside world knows nothing. The signature is clear, and

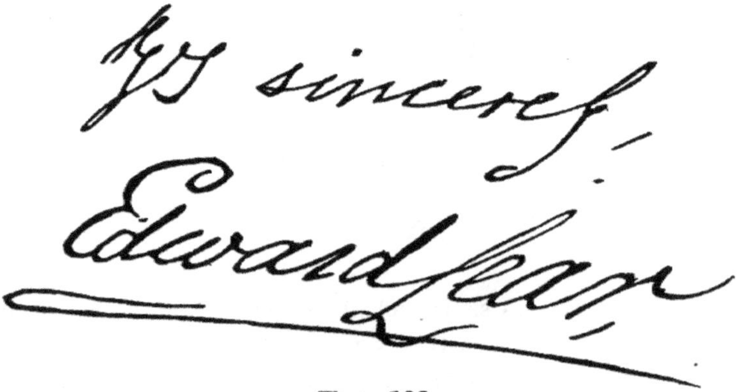

FIG. 100.

shows gentleness and tenderness, and a total absence of all subterfuge, the last letter being even larger than those in the commencement of the word. Subtle and crafty natures are indicated by the reverse of this, as we have shown in our remarks on Dissimulation. The letter is, as we have said, a bright and playful one, and as it is not of a private nature, and may interest our readers, we transcribe it:

"My dear, —I had hoped to be in town so as to come to yon by your usual dinner hour, but some people are coming to lunch to-morrow whom I greatly want to see, so that I shan't be able to get to town so early; instead therefore of 6.30, will you kindly cajole the cheerful cook to serve the salubrious soup at 7?"

"If this cannot be, please put a mutton chop under the sideboard, and I will eat it meekly, in token of repentance for giving trouble for nothing."

Then comes a little playful sketch in pen and ink of himself eating the said chop, and the signature we have given. The brightest and gayest people are often the victims of despondency. We have not the pleasure of knowing Mr. Lear, and we have never seen any other signature of his; but this offers so remarkable an instance of the downward tendency in a signature that we have been tempted to copy it.

Our third example (Fig. 101.) is a fac-simile of the unfortunate Queen Marie Antoinette's signature, from a letter written when she was in prison and under sentence of death. We have seen other signatures of hers at an earlier period in which the signature was straight, but mis- fortune, separation from her husband and children, and humiliation had crushed her pride, and the whole signature is descendant, and the four last letters remarkably so. There is still, however, something

Fig. 101.

regal— something of the daughter of Maria Theresa in the absolute way in which the letter "t" is barred; the letter "m" too, has a certain force —poor, imprisoned, doomed to death on the scaffold, the discrowned queen still signs regally and majestically without any of the vulgar pretentious flourishes in which the lower natures are apt to indulge.

Minutia or attention to detail, is shown by a great regard to punctuation combined with the sign typical of prudence or caution, that of putting a line at the end of almost every sentence and under the signature. It is also indicated by a writing which is upright, and compressed. Our example (Fig. 102) is taken from a letter of Adam White, Esq., Entomologist, British Museum. We cannot tell the date of this letter, as we have only a part of it. Our readers will here see the man of detail and accuracy, on even the smaller points of an assertion, in the neat, clear, but compressed writing; there is not the slightest indication of imagination or fancy. Order is here dominant; not an "i" appears undotted, not a "t" unbarred, all the stops are there, and at the close of the sentence we have not only the full stop, but a line is added, and

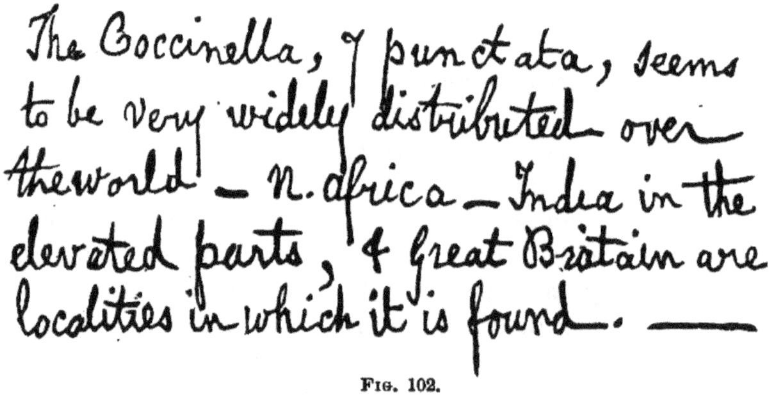
The Coccinella, 7 punctata, seems
to be very widely distributed over
theworld — N. Africa — India in the
elevated parts, & Great Britain are
localities in which it is found. ——

Fig. 102.

this extreme precision goes on through the whole page of information. Originality is a quality the signs of which somewhat resemble those which indicate imagination; but the calligraphist must be careful to distinguish between the characteristics of each in a handwriting, or his judgment will sometimes be wide of the mark. In the writing of almost all imaginative persons we shall find the signs typical of originality; for, imagination being the creative power of the mind, a person gifted with it will always possess a certain originality of thought, and this will be evidenced in his writing, although the signs significative of imagination will probably be dominant; but, as many original persons are not at all imaginative, we shall probably come a cross handwriting in which originality, or individuality, will be very much marked, whilst the signs typical of imagination will be totally absent.

Our readers will remember that we said the signs of imagination are—first, the long flying up strokes and down strokes; and, secondly, the peculiarly large-headed but graceful capitals. Originality runs imagination close in its outward sign of the peculiar forms of letters; and, in that they are peculiar and erratic, they give to the writing that untidy illegibility which, we have said, is the result of the predominance in a handwriting of the signs typical of imagination; but the great difference is that, whilst the eccentric forms peculiar to the poetic or imaginative mind are shown in the writing which is typical of originality, the graceful and flowing forms are entirely absent.

In Fig. 103, which is a fac-simile of the signature of Cruikshank, the artist, we have extreme origiality in every letter, without any sign of the imaginative quality, which is, however, a little shown by the long upstrokes and downstrokes in the rest of the letter from which this is taken. However, the whole of the writing is characterised by the signs typical of originality or marked individuality, and the signature most remarkably so. We would call our readers' attention first to the peculiar form of the small letter "e" in the abbreviation of the Christian name; next, to the eccentric movement of the pen before the capital "C" is

Fig. 103.

formed; and, finally, to the large size of the letter "k" in both instances where it occurs, and to the peculiar termination given to the last. We have seen another signature of Cruikshank's which, while equally original, indeed, presenting all the points we have just noticed, had besides an inordinate flourish beneath the name; but as this is the only one of his signatures which we have seen so disfigured (all the others being like that we have given) we came to the conclusion that the pretentious flourish (quite unworthy of so clever an artist) must have been done in some special moment of self glorification, and we have therefore given him the benefit of the doubt by choosing as our specimen the simple signature, which is the one we have most often seen appended to his letters.

71

In our second example (Fig. 104), the signature of Mr. Buskin
(taken from a letter written some ten or twelve years since to a young
lady friend) we have originality very much marked, but imagination
almost equally so. Originality is shown in the initial of the Christian
name, which is eccentric but not graceful, and imagination, in a great
degree, in the large-headed flowing and gracefully formed capital "E "
at the head of the name; originality again shows itself in the small letter

Fig. 104.

"k," which is large enough to do duty for a capital letter. In our third
and last example, Fig. 105 (the signature of Mrs. Thistlethayte, the
celebrated lady preacher of some years ago), we have originality in the
form of the initial of the Christian name; in the form of the capital "T,"
which is very eccentric; in the tall letter "t," which is much higher than
the upstroke of the "h" which follows it; also in the crooked form of
the downstroke of the small letter "y," and the termination of the letter

Fig. 105.

"e" at the end of the name. There is a total absence of will throughout this handwriting; not a "t" is crossed or even looped; imagination
of the erratic, ill-governed order is shown by the long up-stokes and
down-strokes, which are all entangled one with another and which,
combined with the absence of any bars or loops to the small letter "t,"
make the handwriting very illegible.

Obstinacy, or, as persons who possess it like to call it, a determined will, is characterised by a handwriting angular and rather upright, and by down strokes terminating abruptly without any return or connecting up stroke; this sign, however, must not be confused with one of the signs typical of economy and avarice. The down-stroke of the obstinate person not only terminates without a return line, like those indicative of the above qualities, but it has a decided thickening at the end, a sort of bludgeon-like termination. The last and strongest indication of the obstinate will is that all the email letters "t" axe barred by a short thick stroke close to the other small letters, and sometimes crushing down upon them. This stroke is sometimes long in the writing of obstinate natures, but then the terminating point has either a sort of angular crook, or it has the same bludgeon-like termination we have indicated as being seen in all the downstrokes of the obstinate person. In our first example of this quality (Fig. 106) we give the signature of the celebrated Dr. Livingstone. The writing here is not very angular, but what force of will is indicated in that thick bar to the letter "t" and equally thick down stroke to the letter "g" There is extreme lucidity of ideas in the clearness of the writing, and frankness is shown by the even size of the letters: no finesse of any sort, and no tenderness, for the writing is rather upright than sloping; there is no vulgar pretentiousness or affectation here; the signature is simple, clear, and devoid of flourish,

Fig. 106.

the dominant characteristic is a doggedly determined will. We have said that one of the signs typical of obstinacy is an angular writing, but still as obstinacy may and does exist very frequently in the characters of gentle and kindly people, so we some- times see the signs of obstinacy (as shown by the bludgeon-like down- stroke and the heavily barred "t"), in conjunction with the sloping lines and rounded curves of the writing of the tender and gentle natures; but then, inasmuch as this gentleness and kindliness will sometimes cause the obstinacy to give way, so the utterly and hopelessly obstinate person is shown rather by the angular upright writing of the harder nature (which is unlikely to be biased by tenderness) in conjunction with the other two signs we have mentioned. The obstinate nature, combined with tenderness and gentleness, is shown in the writing we give (Fig. 107.), which is taken from a French letter we have recently received, and of which we have coped a line, which illustrates what we have said. Our readers will notice ^the sloping direction of the writing, indicative of tenderness, and that some of the curves are rounded, though some are angular. The obstinacy is shown by the short, thick downstroke of the letter "q" in the word "que," thicker at its termination than at the commencement, and the heavy bars to the letter "t" in both instances where it occurs,

Fig. 107.

terminating in the first instance in the bludgeon-like form; in the second in the heavy crook which we have indicated as another sign typical of obstinacy, and which is here so large that it runs into the accent (grave) over the letter "e" in the last word *ministère*.

Penetration is shown, in a handwriting, by the same signs as we have given as indicative of intuitive judgment—viz., letters in juxtaposition, without any connecting lines between them. We have seen a signature of Michelet, the author of those interesting and exquisitely written works, "La Femme" and "L'Oiseau"—the latter full of minute and graphic descriptions of nature—in which each letter of the autograph stood by itself; this invariably means penetration, observation, and a rapid or intuitive judgment.

Patience is indicated by the same signs as those typical of minutia, compression—only in a patient person the letters have generally rounded curves, as in this example, and the quality of patience need not have the signs of caution, which are always seen in combination in a character given to minutia or detail.

Perseverance, again, has the same signs as patience, only with them the writing of a persevering person takes a persistently ascendant movement; for perseverance is *patience combined* with energy and action, both of which are moderated by an *ascendant* writing.

Reminfement of mind, and consequently of manners, is shown

by a writing in which delicacy and grace are predominant; the writing of a refined person will also have thes ign of tenderness or sensitiveness strongly deve- loped. This will be seen in the example we give (Fig. 108.), which is the writing of an old lady, now in her 76th year, a person of the utmost refinement. Our readers will notice the softly sloping lines of the writing, and the extreme grace of the capital letters. There is always a certain neatness in

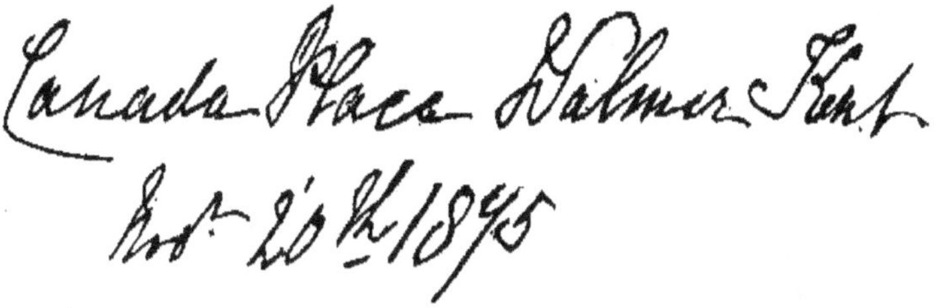

Fig. 108.

the writing of refined persons, unless indeed they are highly imaginative, when the more active quality (imagination) will assert itself, and, while the grace and delicacy of form peculiar to cultivation and refinement will remain, the long flowing upstrokes and downstrokes and somewhat erratic movement given by the fervour of imagination, will a little interfere with the neatness, which is one of the characteristics of refinement where it exists without imagination in the writer. We cannot resist again warning our readers to bear in mind these combinations of qualities, and also to remember that in judging a hand they must always take into consideration (when a hand shows qualities which, without being really contradictory in themselves, are yet so in their characteristic signs) which quality of the two is of the more active nature, and hence more likely, without being at all in greater excess in the character, to dominate the indications of a hand- writing. In the example we have given we have kindliness and tenderness to a great degree, but no imagination; hence the dominant feature is its refinement, without any disturbing element of impatience, ardour, or imagination. The sensitive tenderness of the nature only increases its refinement.

In speaking of dissimulation we warned our readers not to compare this quality with that of subtlety of mind, or as the French render it finesse. Dissimulation, as we have said, is shown in tortuous lines, in letters of uneven heights and in words which are gladiolated, that is, which begin large, but invariably run smaller to the end. Now finesse, or that subtlety of mind which distinguishes the clever person, has one indication which we have given as marking the dissimulative person: the words are gladiolated, but the distinctive mark between the qualities is, that where the dissimulating person writes with a serpentine waviness of line the clever straightforward person, who only wishes to be successful in life, without injuring others, although using the gladiolated words, invariably writes in straight lines. In the specimen (Fig. 109.) which we give of this quality, which is the writing of one very dear to us, we would call our readers' attention to the extreme straightness of the lines, typical of perfect honesty of purpose, and to the sloping movement of the letters, showing tenderness and affectionateness; there are also evidences of will in the way in which the small letters "t" are barred, but not an obstinate will, merely enough to give force of character to the delicate tracery of the writing. If our readers will turn back to the example we gave of dissimulation and compare the two hands, they will at once see the force of what we advance. Whilst the words of the example of dissimulation are almost illegible, these are clear as day. There is no wish to deceive or trick another here; the writer wishes to arrive cleverly at her ends, and always did so, but she would never have been guilty of the lightest act of injustice to anyone.

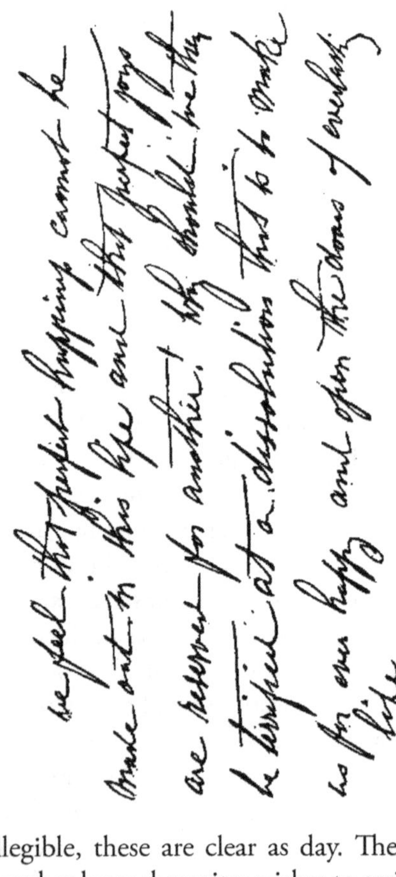

Fig. 109.

We have had such frequent occasion to speak of the sign typical of tenderness and sensitiveness, that, now we have come to the quality in alphabetical order, it seems almost needless to say that tenderness is indicated by a writing which is very sloping; the rounded curves indicative of gentleness and sweetness generally exist with the sloping handwriting, but not always. In our first example (Fig. 110), which is from a private letter of the late Dowager Queen Adelaide, the wife of William IV. to a young goddaughter, we have a fine specimen of sensitive tenderness, combined with imagination, as shown in the long upstrokes and downstrokes, in many instances running into the letters above and beneath them, and thus giving illegibility to a hand which, in other respects, shows great clearness. The signature is spoiled by the absurd amount of flourish, but there is originality in the peculiar form of the capital "A" in the signature; there is very little strength of will in this writing; the small letters "t" are looped, not barred, and even the loops are but feebly indicated.

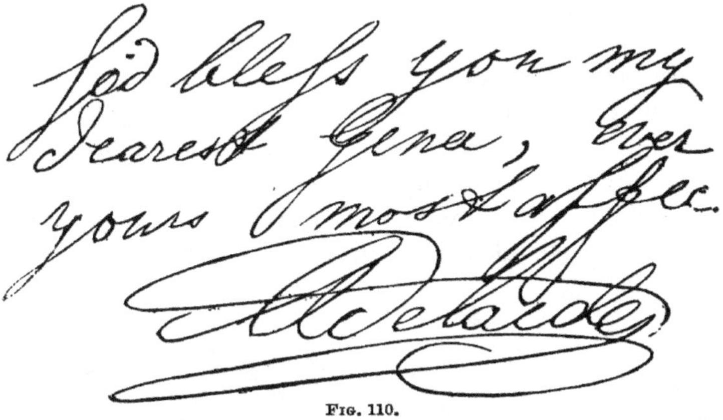

FIG. 110.

Our second example (Fig. 111) of the quality of tendernessis the signature taken from a familiar letter to a Mrs. Fane, written by Mrs. S. C. Hall.

We do not remember ever to have met with a handwriting more thoroughly characteristic of extreme tenderness than this of Mrs. Hall's, and, we think that our readers will agree with us. The long upstrokes and downstrokes which, in many parts of the body of the letter, get quite entangled with the words above and beneath, show a vivid imagination; and the very ascendant movement of the writing indicates ardour, hope, and ambition; there is great grace in the forms of some of the capitals, especially in that of the letter "H" in the signature.

FIG. 111.

The indications of the different shades of will—whether arbitrary, choleric, persevering, or obstinate—are all given by the manner in which the letter "t" is formed. From the simple letter, without bar or even loop, indicative (as is also the long feeble bar growing fine to its termination) of the absolute want of will in a character—to the enormous thick and squarely terminating bars of the strong and obstinate will, this letter is capable of expressing all the gradations of will; but, as we have said in treating of obstinacy (which, after all, is but a strong will in an unreasoning nature), the combination of an angular form of the letter will always increase the force of the demonstration of will as shown in barring or non-barring of the letter "t."

When the letter is barred very strongly, and with along line terminating in a stroke thicker than the commencement, it is a sign of

FIG. 112.

tenacious, but not choleric, will. In Fig. 112, which is the fac-simile of a signature on a franked letter from H. Stuart Wertley, written in 1811, we have this form of the bar, and, taken in conjunction with the angular form of the letters and the thick bar of the down stroke of the letter "y" at the end of the signature, we should say that Mr. Stuart Wortley must have been a man whose will was as immutable as the laws of the Medes and Persians. There is a gleam of hope, however, for the possible

78

yielding of his wishes to a person he eared for, in the extremely sloping direction of the writing. His tenderness might make him occasionally yield, in spite of his will; but where indifference was felt he must have been a provoking man to deal with. There is finesse indicated by the gladiolated form of the surname of the last three letters, "l," "e," and "y" being much smaller than those of the beginning of the word, the "l" being even of less important height than the letter "t" which precedes it. The bars of the small letter "t" long and flying upwards mean a quick, choleric will, arbitrary only for the moment, but capable of being modified by reason when the anger has passed. Of this order

Fig. 113.

of will we give a specimen in Fig. 113, which is the fac-simile of the signature of Admiral Sir John Beresford Rolte, on a letter which bears post date 1822; this sort of vivacious hot tempered will is often seen in the handwriting of distinguished military and naval men. It goes with the ardent energetic temperament, which leads to a man's

Seeking the bubble reputation
Even in the cannon's mouth.

We hive noticed it in the writing of Lord Lucan, in that of Nelson, and in the writing of many of the French generals.

In Fig. 114 (a fac-simile of an autograph of the Earl of Thanet on a franked letter, postmark 1816), we have a specimen of the total absence of will combined with egotism: the long flourishing loop, not bar, to the terminating "t" of the signature, shows want of will in its careless loose line, but a considerable amount of self assertion in its long flourish, which cuts even the initial letter of the name; but for the indications of tenderness in the sloping direction of the letters, we should say that the man who thus signed was a feeble-minded egotist whose first thought in everything was himself.

The letter "t," barred very high and quite at the summit of the letter— indeed, sometimes flying far above it—means a quick and despotic will.

In Fig. 115, taken from & fac-simile of a word in the writing of the late Emperor Nicholas of Russia, we have a good example of this despotic will; it is the word "tant" (the Emperor generally wrote in French), and our readers will notice how the thick line which does duty for both letters "t" flies above the letters to which it belongs.

A bar of the same character, that is long and thicker at the end

Fig. 114.

Fig. 115.

than at its commencement, but crushed down upon the letters, and even cutting the tops of those on a line with it, means an arbitrary and obstinate will, the very worst possible combination. We have this quality shown in a remarkably salient manner in Fig. 116; the word we give is taken from a letter we received from a would be tenant of ours; we felt as we looked at the letter (throughout which every bar was crushed down upon (the letters beneath), that this person would not be pleasant to deal with in any sort of negotiation, and we were not sorry when we found, from certain stipulations which we could not carryout, that there would be no need for further correspondence. The angularity of the forms of the letters, and the heavy bludgeon-like termination to the downstroke of the letter "J," increase the significance of the character given by the peculiar form of the bar.

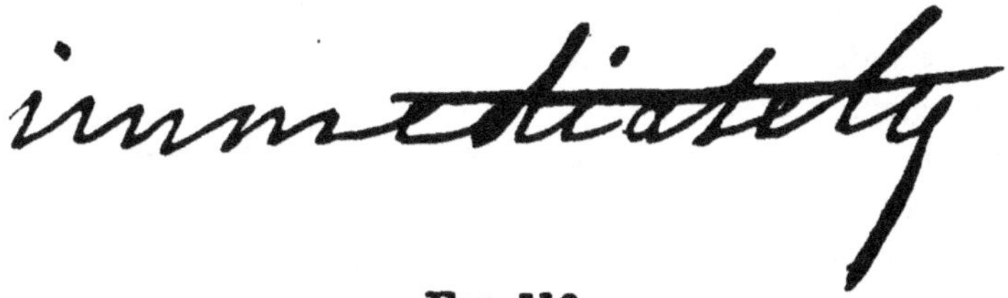

Fig. 116.

The short thick bar to the letter "t," also means obstinacy of the slow dull sort, and is generally seen in a handwriting where there is not the slightest indication of imagination; it means the slow, dull obstinacy of the thoroughly unreasoning mind, which is incapable of seeing more than one side of a question, or of altering the point of view from which a subject has been first considered; it is generally seen in a handwriting which is very even, in which there is no finesse, no intuitive judgment (for this last goes with quicker moving minds), and, as we have said, no imagination. We do not happen to have a specimen of this sort of barred "t" by us, but from our description our readers will be able to recognise it when they see it. Zeal is a combination of the qualities which we gave as being characteristic of loyalty, only energy and ardour must be more dominant than even tenderness, which is one of the most salient features in a handwriting which typifies loyalty. Caution is generally absent; it was for this reason, perhaps, that Talleyrand added, after giving his instructions to one of his myrmidons, "Et surtout point de zèle." Talleyrand, probably, in his worldly wisdom, thought

> The loyalty, well held to fools, does make
> Our faith mere folly.

We ourselves confess to having a great weakness for natures in which the qualities which are typical of loyalty are dominant. To us there is nothing more touching than this "mere folly," and so the great master probably thought himself, for he instantly corrects the coldness of the sarcasm by adding:

> Yet that can endure
> To follow with allegiance a fallen lord,
> Does conquer him that did his master conquer,
> And earns a place i' the story.

81

Having finished what we consider to be the explanation of our theory of judgment of character from handwriting, we now offer a few autographs by way of addenda to the work, as by them we think we shall be able to demonstrate the correctness of the theory—in fact, we offer them as the proof of the sum we have been endeavouring to work out in these pages. We shall give specimens of the signatures of the poets, of distinguished military and naval men, of statesmen and of painters and musicians; and we think we shall be able to show that, among the poets the signs typical of imagination and originality will be dominant; among the military and naval men, ardour and energy; among statesmen, clearness of thought, acuteness and finesse, amounting sometimes to dissimulation, as will be seen in the signature of Talleyrand, the diplomatist, of whose autograph we are enabled to give our readers a fac-simile.

Place aux poetes—the kings amongst men—and highest among the highest, we place first on the page, Shakespeare (Fig. 117). In this signature, we find as we should have expected, imagination and originality dominant, more especially in the letters of the surname, in which, by the way we have noticed that the most marked individuality in a signature always shows itself, and this will be readily understood; for instance, there are many Williams in the world, but, alas! few Shakespeares. Strong intuitive observation—that quick movement of the mind, which seizes character at a glance—is shown by the want of liaison between the curiously formed letter "h" and the "a" which follows it. This quality, too, one should have expected to find, for even the

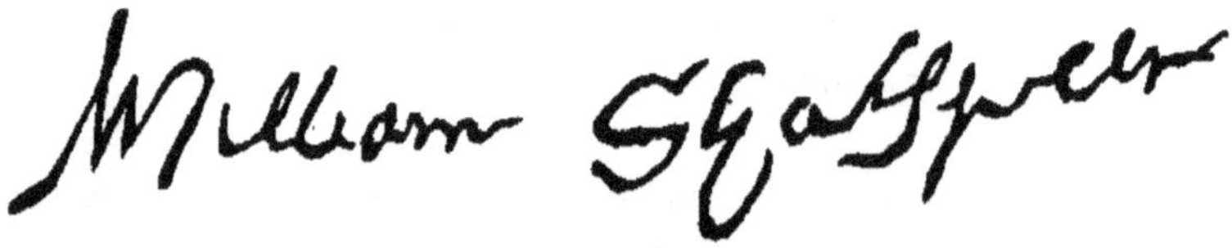

FIG. 117.

young gentleman in Punch, who "thought Shakespeare a very much over-rated man," would, we think, have allowed the poet to have possessed observation in a very remarkable degree. With a poet's disregard of order, Shakespeare puts no dots to either of the small letters "i " in his Christian name, nor is there any full stop at the end of the signature, so suggestive, when seen in an autograph, of caution, and that attention to minutia which seems almost incompatible with the poetic nature. No flourish of any kind disgraces this thoroughly characteristic signature of England's greatest poet.

In Fig. 118 wehave the signature of Sydney Dobell, the writer of the pathetic poem "Bolder," many of the lines in which are exquisite in pathos. Imagination here again is dominant—tenderness is shown in the soft rounded curves of the letters in the surname.

In Fig.119 we have the signature of Longfellow. Here again we have imagination in the letter "L" in the signature of the surname; lucidity of ideas in the extreme clearness of the writing, but not as much tenderness as one would have expected in the writing of the author of "Evangeline."

In Fig. 120, we have the signature of the Laureate; poetic feeling is shown in the graceful form of the capital letter "A," and also in that of the letter "T;" tenderness in the sloping direction of the writing, but not as fervid an imagination as we notice in the signature of Sydney Dobell.

Fig. 121, the signature of Gerald Massey: Immense imagination in the form of the letter "G," tenderness in some of the rounded curves and sloping direction, and that natural tendency to depression, which one often finds among the poets, is indicated by the running down of the three last letters of the signature.

In Fig. 122 we have the signature of Victor Hugo, better known in England, perhaps, by his prose writings. His novels of "Les Misérables" and "The Hunchback of Notre Dame," have been read by many English

FIG. 118.

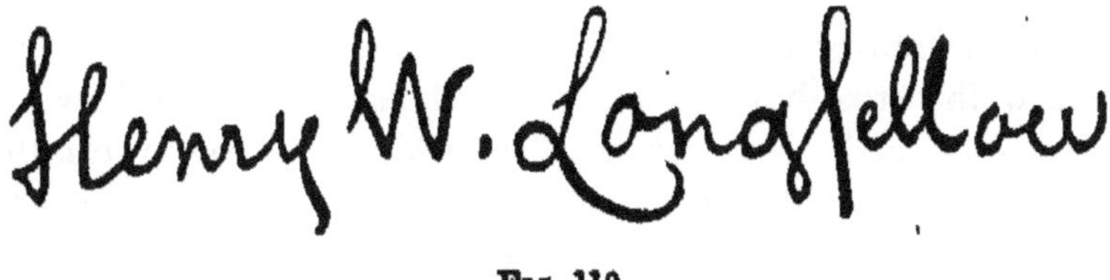

FIG. 119.

83

persons to whom his exquisite lyrics are unknown; but he is essentially the poet. We would draw our readers' attention to the imagination indicated by the large flowing form of the capital "V," and to the excessive development of the downstroke of the small letter "g" in the word Hugo, a sign, this, of an imagination of the most fervid order. There is

FIG. 120.

FIG. 121.

FIG. 122.

FIG. 123.

power in the form of the letter " H," and the wide space between the two strokes of the letter shows boldness and self dependence. We drew our readers' attention in the signature of Henry V. of France (known as the Comte de Chambord), to the extreme compression of the two strokes, a sign of want of force of character, and of constraint; there is none of that here—misfortune, loss of a dearly loved son, exile—nothing has been able to repress this ardent nature. Like Shakespeare, he has a soul above the dotting of the letter "i." Intuitive observation too, here, as in Shakespeare, is indicated: the letter "i" stands quite apart from the capital "V" which precedes it and from the letter "o" which follows it. This is the sign typical, as we have said, of intuitive observation and judgment, and when seen, either in the writing of poets or men of science, it means the power of seizing at once the different aspects of things; a sort of (if one may be allowed the expression) spontaneous conception. Space prevents our giving further examples of the poets, although we should gladly have done so; but we have given sufficient for the theory, and we now pass on to the signatures of our naval and military men.

Fig. 123. The signature of Lord Nelson when captain. Ardour and ambition in the mounting character of the whole signature. The tenderness, an excess of which drew him into error, is also evident in the eloping direction of the writing. A beautiful and interesting signature.

Fig. 124. The signature of Marshal Soult, the fiery French general. Here we have the same indications of ardour and ambition, an ascended writing, and the bar of the letter "t," like that in Nelson's signature, flying upwards, denoting ardour to an almost foolhardy disregard of life.

FIG. 124.

FIG. 125.

Fig. 125. The signature of Lord Raglan, when Lord Fitzroy Somerset. Not quite so ascendant a writing as the other two; but still the movement is rather upwards than not, and ardour is also indicated by the long upward stroke with which the name terminates.

In Fig.126 we have a most interesting signature—that of the fiery Condé, one of the most ardent and impetuous of the French military heroes. Could anything be more rampantly mounting than this signature? His ardour makes him forget the capital to his surname, which he writes, it will be remarked, all in one, instead of "De Bourbon"—a simple and noble signature, however, and quite without any pretentious flourish of any sort.

In Fig. 127, the writing of General Sir Hew Dalrymple, the same-mounting movement will be observed. We have been unable to procure the signature of the Duke of Welington; but our readers have already had a specimen of the Iron Duke's writing amongst the fac-similes we gave illustrative of ambition, and they will remember, perhaps, the vaulting character of the writing throughout the note of which we gave the fac-simile.

FIG. 126.

FIG. 127.

In Fig. 128, we have a fac-simile of the signature of Sir Robert Peel taken from a letter franked by him. The most remarkable point in this auto- graph is its extreme clearness, indicative of lucidity of ideas. Cultivation is shown in the graceful form of the capital letters to both

Christian and surname, and sequence of ideas in the liaison between the small letter "b" (which terminates the abbreviation of the Christian name) and the capital "P" of the surname. This joining of the small letter to the capital is remarkable, as the Christian name i3 written in abbreviation, in which case it is usual to put some sign of the abbrevi-

FIG. 128.

ation between it and the surname. Lastly, extreme straightforwardness is indicated in this signature, the letters are all of one height, and the line of the writing is straight as a dart; it is, in our opinion, a noble and beautiful signature, worthy of the man of whom his Queen held a high opinion.

In Fig. 129, which we have given at the fame time as the signature of the straightforward English statesman, we give that of Prince Talleyrand, the great French diplomatist, who was once heard to say, in the intimacy of a small circle, "On doit avoir pour principe de ne jamais écrire; on peut nier avoir dit une chose et nul ne vous prouvera matériellement que vous l'avez dite mais l'écriture reste toujours là." Of course this was said apparently in mere jest, but we have but to glance at the tortuous, almost illegible signature, with its small, compressed letters (the terminating "d" so gladiolated as to look more like a small letter "o" than the letter it was intended to represent) to feel quite sure that the writer sought to make his writing as impenetrable as his

FIG. 129.

spoken words; but, to the calligraphist, this very effort defeats its end. Research has shown us that this serpentine line, this irregularity, in the size of the letters will be found (in a more or less degree) in the writing of all the men who have distinguished themselves in diplomatic states-manship. In none, however, have we seen it more pronounced than in the handwritings of Talleyrand, Cavour, Louis Philippe, and Louis Napoleon. Talleyrand's writing, in the short extract from a letter to which this signature was appended, shows also ardour, ambition, and perseverance—all these qualities he possessed in an eminent degree. There is an utter absence of all flow and movement —no large headed graceful letters indicative of imagination, none of the fine flowing curves suggestive of generosity and expansion—all is com- pressed and impenetrable as the man himself.

We pass on to another contrast, the signature (Fig. 130) of Lord Falmerston when he was in the zenith of his power. How well the kindly genial temperament of the popular minister is shown in the rounded curves of the three last letters of the name. We have also cultivation and originality in the form of the capital letter; a temperate will in the steady, but not hard, bar to the small letter "t." No obstinacy; only sufficient firmness to hold his own where necessary, a man open to con-victions from this absence of obstinacy, combined with the acuteness of observation shown in the angular form of the capital letter. There

Fig. 130.

is a certain mounting movement indicative of energy if not ambition; though it is, perhaps, hardly vaulting enough for that to be considered a salient quality in the signature.

In Fig. 131, we have the signature of Proudhon, the great French economist and politician of the Second Empire. Here we have all the ardent imagination, which made Proudhon play so great a part in the movement of ideas during the Second Empire. This signature is inter-esting, as being so characteristic of all we know of Proudhon in his writ-ings, that we have been induced to give it, although, as a rule, we prefer to give examples of English handwritings. It seemed, however, to us so natural and spontaneous a signature that we could not resist giving it. It is taken from a letter to one of his intimate friends, to whom he had written hurriedly, asking advice on a little matter of business. Imagination is, as we have said, here dominant in the large headed capitals, and after imagination, which is one of the qualities most remarkable in his works, we have another force—a marked individuality and self-assertion in the enormously long nourish at the termination of the name. As a rule, the signatures of the highest and most poetic natures, whilst imagination is dominant, are yet quite without this nourish of self-assertion, but we invariably see it developed in the signatures of men who have made themselves popular, and it denotes a certain force, though

FIG. 131.

not delicacy, of nature. This sort of fervid imagination combined with the self-assertion, is what one generally sees in the signatures of popular orators, and Proudhon, in his works, was really more of an orator than a thinker, he knew how to make the hearts of the people vibrate in his works as though they were spoken words; it is, however, in "La Justice dans la Revolution et'dans l'Eglise," that Proudhon's ardent imagination and originality most show themselves.

In Fig. 132 we have the signature of the great Lord Thurlow—extreme force of character and imagination in the capital letter, acuteness and strong will in the angular form of the letters. This characteristic of acutness is to be seen in the writing of most great lawyers; in Fig. 133 (Lord Brougham's signature), it is the salient 1 feature, as it is also in that of Lord Denman (Fig. 134), and in that of Lord Erskine (Fig. 135), but in this last we have also cultivation and refinement in the graceful form of the capital "E."

We have shown imagination to be the salient quality in the hand-writing of the poets, and the sign typical of it is always to be found in a more or less degree in the writing of all painters and sculptors of eminence; indeed, the handwritings of poets and artists are so similar in their characteristics that it is always difficult to say with certainty to which art the writer has given himself, and this will be readily under-stood. Painting and poetry are but the different modes of expression of the same nature, circumstances very frequently being the motive power which decides by which voice the fervid imagination and sense

FIG. 132.

FIG. 133.

FIG. 134.

FIG. 135.

of beauty peculiar to both the poetic and artistic nature expresses itself. The musician, too, being of the same temperament, only with less intellectual power than the poet and artist, will have somewhat of the characteristics, which distinguish the other two in his writing.

As a rule, we should mark the differences thus: whilst the poet has more imagination and originality, the artist, with both these qualities in a less degree, will have the perception of beauty of form (indicated by the grace of the capitals) to a greater degree than the poet—whilst the musicians, with less imagination and sense of beauty of form, will have tenderness more strongly developed. However, of this and of the difference between the composer and the mere executive musician, we shall speak farther on.

In Fig. 136 we have the signature of Sir Francis Grant. Great imagination is shown in the large head and equally large base of the capital letter "F;" here is originality in the form of the capital "G," and a certain tenderness in the sloping direction of the writing.

In Fig. 137 we have the signature of the celebrated sculptor David. Immense imagination in the capital letter "D," at the head of the signature, sense of form in the clear lines of the letter, but not much tenderness. The signature is rather spoiled, in our estimation, by the egotism and self assertion indicated by the absurd flourish at its termination;

Fig. 136.

still, it must be taken into consideration that it is a Frenchman's signature, and one rarely sees this quite devoid of some sort of flourish. As we said in our opening remarks, there are national as well as individual characteristics in handwriting, and, in judging of the individual, the graphologist must bear this in mind. The French, as a people, are vain, boastful, and self assertive, and the national handwriting shows this as well as its good qualities, such as grace, sensitiveness, and tenderness. In order to prove what we have just said as regards the French habit of flourishing roundabout a signature, we give that of the French painter

Fig. 137.

91

Flandrin (Fig. 138). Now an Englishman of the same eminence in his art would never have surrounded his signature with such a hideous oblong flourish. Nothing but the utmost egotism and self assertion could have induced any one with no decided a sense of beauty of form as his capital letter "H" indicates, to disfigure his signature thus. We have in this writing an exquisite tenderness as marked as what we generally find in a musician's hand. Great sense of beauty is indicated (as we have said) by the graceful form of the capital letter "H," and this Flandrin had; his style was perfected by his close study of Raphael.

Fig. 138.

There is not much imagination in this signature, but the creative power given by imagination is not very observable in his works, whilst sense of beauty is remarkably so; hence his great admiration for Raphael.

As our last example of the artist's writing, we give one of De Wint (Fig. 139), where sense of beauty 'and tenderness [are the salient points. The first shewn in the graceful and flowing form ;of the capitals; the last in the sloping direction of the writing. The want of force of this signature is somewhat corrected by the strong hard line drawn under the name; this does not indicate (as a, flourish does) self assertion and egotism, but force of character, and a certain amount of caution, when, like in this example, the line is firm and straight; a wavy line under the name with a rounded and mounting termination partakes of the character of a flourish, but the straight hard line indicates, as we have said,

Fig. 139.

force, decision, and, above all, caution. We have, however, seen other signatures of De Wint's without this line, and with less decision in the writing. This signature was possibly that to some letter on business of importance. We did not see the letter to which it was appended, as the signature only was lent us for our purpose. As the handwriting of poets and artists is similar, so likewise is that of doctors and lawyers, and here again it will be admitted that the resem- blance is most natural. Both lawyers and doctors have to exercise the faculties of penetration and clearness of ideas. We have already pointed out how all the signatures of the great lawyers were remarkable for the indications of acuteness, many by the angular form of the letters, and the extreme clearness of the hand, typical of lucidity of ideas.

In Fig. 140, which is the signature of the celebrated Sir Astley Cooper, our readers will remark at once its salient point as being that of extreme clearness. Sequence of ideas (also very natural to find in a great doctor) is indicated by the curious liaison of the bar of the letter "t" to the head of the capital "C " in the surname.

In Fig. 141, the signature of Chambers, we have the same clearness and the same sequence of ideas, the latter shown by the joining of the loop of the capital letter "W" to the letter "T " of the other initial. The angular form, denoting penetration, is not so marked as in Sir Astley Cooper's writing, but there are indications of it in the two initial capital letters before the surname.

FIG. 140.

In giving the signatures of the musicians, that of Beethoven (Fig. 142) seems to us to stand as preeminently forward as that of Shakespeare among the poets. Let our readers turn back to the signature of the greatest of poets, and compare it with that of what we (as we are certainly not Wagnerists) consider that of the greatest musician, and he will be at once struck with the similarity of the handwriting; the same fire and fervour of imagination is shown in Beethoven's signature by the peculiar form of the capital letter B as in Shakespeare's by that

Fig. 141.

Fig. 142.

of the letter S; there is the same movement in the writing indicative of passion and originality. The minds of the two men must have been almost alike, but the fact that the one possessed the gift of sensitiveness to sound more than the other, forced him to give expression to the creative force within him in music rather than in the still more intellectual art of poetry. As, however, the first art gives more universal pleasure than the other (for there are few people, even the stupidest, who are not moved by the "concord of sweet sounds"), we must not regret that nature having gifted Beethoven with the "ear for music" as it is called, we received a great musician rather than a second Shakespeare—since to the world at large this was, perhaps, the greater gift. The tenderness so peculiar to musicians is visible here; but the fire and passion always to be noticed in the signatures of the composers prevents the tenderness from being as marked as it is in the signatures of mere executive musicians, where there is not so much imagination to stir the sweet serenity of the simply tender nature.

Our readers will notice in Beethoven's signature the same distinctive mark of high genius which we remarked upon in that of Shakespeare—there is no flourish whatsoever; he is just simply himself; no need for any flourish of self-assertion. And this is even more remarkable in the foreigner than in the Englishman, for, as we have before observed, few foreigners sign without some addenda of this sort. We have seen a signature of Dumas, the French novelist, in which the signature was not only surrounded, but almost rendered illegible, by the amount of flourish around, above, and below it; but then Dumas, though a very clever writer, was certainly a genius of second-rate order—great in his class, perhaps, but certainly not one of the 4lite. Side by side with this disfigured signature we saw, in the same collection of autographs, that of Pension, the author of that most exquisitely poetic, but now little-read work, "Télémaque." Never did we see a nobler signature; poetry, tender-grace, all were there, as markedly as in his works, and, above all, noble simplicity and unpretentiousness, the absence of all flourish, which distinguishes the truly great mind.

Fig. 143. which is that of Spontini, an Italian composer, whose works were much admired in their time by some people, we have a mind of a very different order, although of no great merit. There is here some originality, but not much, shown by the peculiar manner of barring the letter "t;" but how wanting is this in the passionate tenderness, the offspring of imagination, which we saw in the preceding signature. Here we have, as we have said, some originality; but it is entirely without imagination, hence of a second-rate order, for none can be truly great in any art where imagination is not the dominating quality. The ugly addenda beneath the name would, in our eyes, spoil a better signature.

FIG. 143.

In our third example (Fig. 144) we have the exquisitely graceful, and therefore truly characteristic, signature of Mendelssohn, which is a fac-simile of the signature appended to a letter addressed by him to Clara Angela, Macirone, the composer, then only a young aspirant for

honours in the art in which he was so great a master. The extreme kindliness of nature shown in this letter, in which, after praising and thank-
ing her for her composition, he expresses a hope that she may "continue
to write many beautiful things," is fully indicated in his handwriting
by its sloping direction, its rounded curves and flowing lines. It is true
this signature has, or appears to have, the very defect we have been
anathematizing above, but "there are flourishes and flourishes." This, it

FIG. 144.

FIG. 145.

FIG. 146.

will be observed, is a continuation of the last letter. Now, small as this
circumstance appears to be, it yet should have weight in our judgment
of character; the flourish that is a continuation of the final letter may
arise from the exuberant fancy of the writer, and denotes the reverse of
economy quite as much as the flourish apart from the name indicates
pretentiousness. This addendum of Mendelssohn is as graceful as any
flourish can be, and when we consider that the signature starts with a
very original and imaginative movement of the pen to form the letter "F," which is, in our eyes, though eccentric, very graceful—we can

96

readily understand that the same pen could hardly bring itself to finish with a quiet upstroke to the " y;" but how graceful the flourish is! We pardon it for its pleasant lines. Apart from this, for which, perhaps (because we love the man in his works), we have been careful to make apology—how beautiful is this signature! How full of that grace which appeared in all he wrote are the capital letters; how sweet, clear,and tender all the smaller letters!

Next in order is the signature of Clara Angela Macirone (Fig. 145). Here we have, in a conspicuous degree, the tenderness which is so marked in all executive musicians of any eminence, and Miss Macirone is one of our first pianists, though she is, perhaps, better known as a composer (which is certainly the higher position), for she has" " continued to write many beautiful things" which, had not the tender heart which was so ready to encourage the promise of her youth been stilled in death, would have been thoroughly appreciated by Mendelssohn. Besides the marked quality of tenderness, we have extreme clearness, as in Mendelssohn, and imagination in the form of the capital. The signature also has that cachet de distinction, the absence of flourish, no pretension, no self assertion, no need for either here. Next in order we give the signature of Kate Loder (Fig. 146), now Lady Thomson, an executive musician and composer. Here we have the same tenderness as in the preceding signature—imagination in the large head of the capital letter "K," and originality in the peculiarity of making the bar of the letter "X" run on to form the first part of the capital letter "L " in the surname.

In Fig. 147 we have that of Lindsay Sloper, the pianist. Tenderness and grace are here dominant. The sense of beauty, necessary in all art, is indicated by the graceful form of the letter "L."

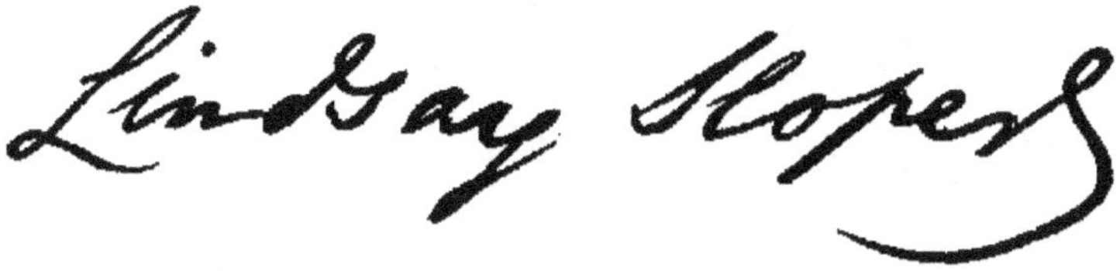

Fig. 147.

In Fig. 148 we give the signature of the musician known to the world as "Beta," under which nom de plume the original and graceful song called "The Mask," so much sung by Miss Dolby, made its appearance. Here, again, tenderness is the most salient quality; but we have

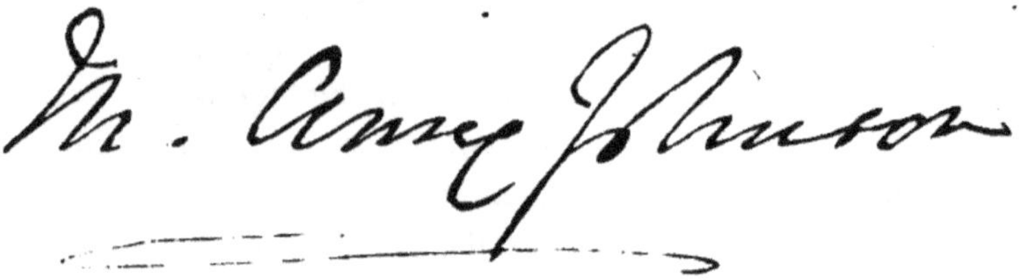

FIG. 148.

also sense of beauty and poetic feeling in the simple form of the letter "A." Imagination is not as much indicated as we should have expected for one who has so well rendered the spirit of Mrs. Browning's pathetic words in "The Mask;" but, probably, had we other capital letters to pass in review, we should find the quality, which is to us the motive power in all art, represented in a more marked manner.

We must apologise to the musicians for giving their signatures so late on our list; but we thought by presenting as our last example names so suggestive of sweet sounds, we should thus be enabled "to make harmonious close."

We have now given our readers the whole of our theory as far as we have completed it ourselves, up to the present moment; but as graphology is a study in which there seems every day something more to learn, they, if they take up the subject, will find that they may readily improve themselves by practice in the art, and in time, perhaps, far outstrip their teacher; and, in order that they may at once put in practice the principles we have laid down, and that, in turn, the critic may be criticised, we beg to submit to them our own signature for judgment whilst subscribing ourselves, theirs very truly,

DISCLAIMER

These letters have never been published before. They were transferred electronically from Pennsylvania State University library
after being taken from their vault. For copyright reasons, these letters
have been deciphered through photos and typed for your reading con-
venience. Some letters and words are illegible and have been replaced
with brackets. These letters may contain errors that were created in the
interpretation process.

A LETTER FROM THE EDITOR

Interpreting these letters was interesting, to say the least; reading
words in cursive that are scattered across a page in a seemingly ran-
dom order was quite the experience. I'm thankful that Penn State was
so accommodating in sending the letters to me.

Reading Broughton's handwriting was like decrypting hiero-
glyphics. She used abbreviations that are no longer relevant, such
as "t" as an abbreviation for "the." The letter "I" resembled a "g" or
occasionally an "S."

My initial reasoning to include these letters after Baughan's book
on handwriting was to exemplify the exact claims Baughan made in her
book. She states that handwriting is affected by one's state of mind and
external factors. Library staff at Pennsylvania State library stated that
these letters are a correspondence between Broughton and a male suit-
or while they were unable to meet for lunch after countless attempts. I
have included only selected letters from the bunch. Though the illegibility of these letters is preventing me from demonstrating that for you,
I think it says just as much that these letters are unable to be read. After
various failed efforts to meet up, we can presume that Broughton's state
of mind was blurry to say the least. This is evident in these letters.

RHODA BROUGHTON LETTERS, CA. 1890

None of the replies are included.

I: 1 MANSFIELD PLACE

My dear
Do come to luncheon tomorrow Thursday the 8th I will try to get my garden facility ready I've forgotten to meet you Send your card to 4th The (location/hotel/house) Bedford

Yours affect [affectionately]
Rhoda Broughton

II:[1]

I've carried to dark with which I have loved Hard choice
[The rest is illegible].

III: 6 ROYAL TERRACE

Dear Mr Radcliffe[2],
You need not have apologized for your very modest request with which I am happy to comply tho I hope that you queried ___ not judge of my character by/of my villainous handwriting. I am writing ___ tour of visits to ride over the __ period of __ my sister is __ing another

June 2

---

1 There were a lot of exclamation points in this letter, seemingly out of despair.
2 The most common recipient of the letters, presumably the male suitor scholars mentioned.

IV: 95 EATON TERRACE

Dear Mr Daniel

My heart is broken!! It has waited to the age of 63 to be ___ed, but
it is now!! I can't come on Saturday as I am engaged to go to Tring
[Trinity] ___ this that happens over in 5 years! I know it ___ came to
dark
With which I _____ have _____ part I met the Lubbock last night,
And he told me _____ were you to ask use; _____ I_____ed
_____ very _____ in luck!! If ___ I would far rather have _____
To you to the _____ ___
I need not answer you of _____.
In _____ _____ your much affection
July? 26th

FURTHER READING
Starry eyed about graphology and divinity?

The Witches' Dream Book and Fortune Teller
by A. H. Noe
1885, H. J. Wehman

A Guide to Palmistry
by Eliza Easter Henderson
2010, Kessinger Publishing, LLC

The Complete Palmist
by Ina Oxenford and A. Alpheus
1902, Kessinger Publishing

A Manual of Cheirosophy: Being a Complete Practical Handbook of the Twin Sciences of Cheirognomy and Chiromancy, by Means Whereof the Past, the Present, and the Future May be Read in the Formations of the Hands; Preceded by an Introductory Argument Upon the Science of Cheirosophy and Its Claims to Rank as a Physical Science
by Ward, Lock, and Bowden
1885, Ward, Lock, and Bowden

Fingers and Fortune: A Guide-book to Palmistry
by Eveline Michell Farwell
1886, David Stott

Handwriting Analysis: The Complete Basic Book
by Karen Kristin Amend
1986, Newcastle Publishing Company

Sex, Lies, and Handwriting
by Michelle Dresbold
2008, Free Press

A Circle of Witches: An Anthology of Victorian Witchcraft Stories
by Peter Haining
1971, Taplinger Pub. Co

A Victorian Grimoire: Romance – Enchantment – Magic
by Patricia Telesco
1992, Llewellyn Publications

The Handbook of Palmistry
by Rosa Baughan
2009 (republished), BiblioLife

Cometh Up as a Flower
by Rhoda Broughton
1867

Not Wisely, But Too Well: A Novel
by Rhoda Broughton
1867

Doctor Cupid
by Rhoda Broughton
1886

Red As A Rose Is She
by Rhoda Broughton
1870